"Part bard, part mystic, and ever diligent walker between the worlds, it's not surprising to find Jesse's words ringing from these pages with visionary clarity—you are called! *Gaia Eros* calls us back to the Mother with honor, respect, integrity, mindfulness, and gratitude as essential guides for our re-awakening."
> —Patricia Telesco, author of
> *Enchanted Life* and coauthor of *God/Goddess*

"Wolf's work is an illuminating personal record...and an invocation of the forthcoming ecological epoch."
> —Peter Berg, director of Planet Drum Foundation

"*Gaia Eros* is a wild ride through the canyons of heart and mind of a modern Earth warrior who has planted himself deeply in his place. Jesse Wolf Hardin writes from the place of true authenticity in an age of superficiality—from his experience and from his soul. I recommend this book to any and all who wish to understand the marriage of magic, activism, spirituality, and service."
> —Jed Swift, ecopsychologist at Naropa Institute

"There is no more important personal awareness, and political movement today, than the strengthening of human communities conscious of place in the natural world. Jesse Wolf Hardin addresses the need of human beings to search within themselves, and within their bioregions, and to make the connections that may save our sanity, and the planet too. I know of no-one more thoughtful or articulate or inspiring."
> —Jerry Mander, author of
> *In The Absence of The Sacred*

"Wolf Hardin offers always a vision of the wild beauty we are a part of, taking us beyond the rational to more deeply felt levels of being. A poet who celebrates our essential sacred, larger living body....he urges us to remember who we are, howl, and celebrate."
—Chris Roth, editor of *Talking Leaves Magazine*

"Such is the power of Wolf's speaking to and for our wilder, vaster, more noble, and joyous selves, that you can expect to see new resolve in anyone fortunate enough to experience him at work for Gaia."
 —Jim O'Connor, founder of Kingsley Wilderness Project

"Fiery...passionate..."
—Paul Winter, world-renowned musician

"Wolf sings us Full Circle to the raw, sweet wildness within, and calls us forward to the future primeval."
—Joanna Macy, author of
World As Self, World As Lover

"His word and voice is the haunting cry of a wild-voiced wilderness seer....the ecstatic song of an Earth lover, a man intoxicated with the beauty and diversity of life. The high-spirited and soulful voices of...the Earth herself, speak and sing through him, reminding us of our ancient heritage of sacred wildness."
—Ralph Metzner, author of
Green Psychology and *Well Of Remembrance;*
founding member, Harzard Psilocybin Project

"His vision is clear and inclusive and his message can take us into the world we are looking to restore and create."
—Sedonia Cahill, coauthor of *The Ceremonial Circle*

"Wolf's loving, erotic sensibility allows him to play on ancient harmonies. He sings us into magician morning, calling us to re-enter primal states of being-in-the-world. He seduces us away from the madness of modern, urban-based civilizations and draws us into the 'great silence,' the way things really are, the Tao. He opens the door of our consciousness and asks us to step out into the fields and mountains. If we are really quiet, Pan comes out of hiding and teaches us the will-of-the-land."

—Bill Devall, author of *Deep Ecology*

"In terms of his depth, personal commitment, and quality of performance, Wolf is peerless. There are few others who have all of his primal qualities. Except for some Aboriginal writers, there are few authors in North America who reflect such depth of being a native to its places—remarkable, given his background as a street kid, with Nordic/Celtic ancestry. He came home to wildness and living close to the Earth. It shows all through his writings and performances. He gives others (such as myself) courage to speak from our own authentic ecological selves. He is a highly productive artisan who is making a most important contribution to the Deep Ecology Movement and a new ecologically responsible culture."

—Prof. Alan Drengson, editor,
The Trumpeter Journal of Ecosophy

"His poetic ruminations illuminate this powerful path to spiritual and environmental peacemaking."

—Jim Nollman, author of *The Charged Border* and
Spiritual Ecology

Gaia Eros

RECONNECTING *to the* MAGIC *and* SPIRIT *of* NATURE

Jesse Wolf Hardin

CPL

NEW PAGE BOOKS
A division of The Career Press, Inc.
Franklin Lakes, NJ

GAIA EROS
EDITED BY KRISTEN PARKES
TYPESET BY EILEEN DOW MUNSON
Cover design by Lu Rossman/Digi Dog Design
Illustration in Prologue by Oberon Zell-Ravenheart
All other interior illustrations by Jesse Wolf Hardin
Printed in the U.S.A. by Book-mart Press

To order this title, please call toll-free 1-800-CAREER-1 (NJ and Canada: 201-848-0310) to order using VISA or MasterCard, or for further information on books from Career Press.

The Career Press, Inc., 3 Tice Road, PO Box 687,
Franklin Lakes, NJ 07417
www.careerpress.com
www.newpagebooks.com

Library of Congress Cataloging-in-Publication Data

Hardin, Jesse Wolf, 1954-
    Gaia Eros : reconnecting to the magic and spirit of nature / by Jesse Wolf Hardin;
    foreword by Amber K; prologue by Oberon Zell-Ravenheart.
        p. cm.
    Includes index.
    ISBN 1-56414-729-0 (pbk.)
        1. Magic. 2. Nature—Miscellanea. 3. Goddess religion. 4. Nature—Religious
    aspects. I. Title.
    BF1623.N35H37 2004
    299--dc22

                                                            2003070231

Acknowledgments

Gratitude goes out first to our primal ancestors, for developing a way of seeing/being/believing that honored self, Earth, and Spirit. Our essential humanity—modes of perception, language, feeling, and values—evolved in close association with the qualities and spirits of the natural world. Over the course of hundreds of thousands of years, these hunters and gatherers, Shamans and healers, dreamers and doers, set a high if imperfect standard for right relationship with the living Earth. They demonstrated how spirituality, magical practice, and ritual could help in keeping our left-brain-dominant species in touch with the inspiration, instructions, gifts, and needs of the natural world of which we're an inextricable part.

Thanks go also to those "Nature mystics" who bucked the ascendant separative cultures of their day, preserving the tradition of Earth-informed spirituality as outlaw poets and backwoods barbarians, priestesses and philosophers, Neo-Druids and magicians. To St. Francis, Walt Whitman, John Muir, Aldo Leopold. And to their contemporary counterparts: passionate Pagans and Unitarians, poets and artists, resolved restorationists and radical scientists, back-to-the-land primitivists and committed communalists, earthy sensualists and community activists, who have contributed to the unification of mind and heart, magic and mission, spirituality and place, personal and social change.

Deep gratitude to the potent priestess and author Amber K for contributing the Foreword to this book, to my wizened wizardly friend Oberon Zell-Ravenheart for the in-depth Prologue, and to the amazing Starhawk for her kind recognition and powerful recommendation. My appreciation to Laurie Kelly, Michael Pye, and the editors of New Page Books for their enthusiastic support...and to the many publications that printed and sometimes provoked portions of the essays found herein, including but not limited to: *Aquarius, Awareness, Circle, Communities, Creations, Earthlight, The Edge, Elements, Evergreen, Gaian Voices, Magical Blend, Mother Earth News, Natural Beauty & Health, New Connexions, One Heart, PagaNet News, PanGaia, Sentient Times,* and *Talking Leaves*

For the sustenance, support, and love that helps make our work and lives possible, I'm especially indebted to John Drake, Dennis Fritzinger, Glenn Henderson, Nick and Sloane Morgan, and Elle and Steve Wilhite. Thank you to sweet, helpful friends Gael and Scott Adams, Scot Deily, Lee Hurwit, Sarah Mace, Glenn Parry of S.E.E.D., Jeff Rosenbaum of Starwood Festival, Sev and Jon Rosseau, Sylvia and Albert, Wendy and Eric. Huge blessings to everyone who has ever helped spread the word about this canyon and Earth-hearted teaching, or whoever will. And my heart goes out to Loba, my love, co-caretaker and co-celebrant for lifetimes to come. The canyon sanctuary, and the world, need your unguarded song.

Finally, thank you to the Seekers of every coming generation, those who will make use of this New Nature Spirituality primer for clarification, inspiration, and grounding in their own time of questioning, challenge, and practice. So much depends on you, on your sometimes agonizing empathy, on your focused and passionate efforts, and on your insistent joy! These insights are threads of Earth wisdom and sacred interconnectedness...and it is to the dedicated weavers of these threads that we must be most thankful of all.

Contents

Foreword

There was a time in every culture when our roots were deep and strong, and not even death could sever them. A time when we belonged so totally to the family, the clan, the tribe, and the land, that the idea of not belonging was unthinkable! We knew who and what we were, in relation to every other person and animal and patch of ground.

In Western society at the dawn of this new millennium, so much of our existence is characterized by separation and alienation. Families shatter and move to the far corners of the nation, and their homes are sold to strangers who have left the places of their own births. Rootless, detached, disconnected, restless, and empty, we numb ourselves to pain and loneliness with the great anesthetics of our day.

Now comes among us a man who not only remembers how it once was, but embodies it still. Jesse Wolf Hardin lives in deep relationship with a river canyon and ancient ritual place of power in the wilds of New Mexico. In that place he thinks deeply, hears Gaia's call, shares in both her suffering and her joy. And best of all, he writes eloquently about it, inspiring our return to a life that is emotionally and spiritually rich, deep, and intimate in its connections with our own feelings, with each other, and with this living planet we call home.

Gaia Eros is about re-learning how to be honest, feeling, aware, sensate human beings, magically co-creating existence and positively influencing events. This is no less than a spiritual understanding, religion in its original sense of re-linking with the inspirited Whole—in this case, through immanent divinity, the holy and sacred all around us and within us.

In these pages you'll discover Earth-given insights about human nature and the natural world, animal totems and plant teachers, vision quests and Gaian wizardry, community and clan. This book redefines attachment and responsibility, explores the meaning of the coming Earth changes, and offers a new way for not only nature lovers and Pagans, but for everyone. Jesse seductively describes the delights of an enchanted kitchen, the power of ceremony and art, and the wonders of the drum, playfully inviting us into the sentient world of sacred indulgence. At the same time, he comes down hard on the fluffy escapism prevalent in the New Age, calling on his readers to do the hard work of re-creating our lives, purchasing and restoring community land, and standing up for what's right as social, political, and environmental activists. He opens with a circle cast wide enough to include every willing seeker...and closes with an ode to adventure, purpose, and risk: "in this grip of dragon-flight! Fly, fly, fly!"

I don't know what part I like best. It could be the soaring voyages into matters of Spirit. It might be the sparse, vivid descriptions of the rocks and rivers he loves. Wolf is the great translator who absorbs the silent truths of the sky and Earth and offers them to us in eloquent human language evoking the heart and intention of Gaia's plaintive message.

Gaia Eros is a book about the magic of such elemental basics as food and sex and shelter: how to savor not only food but existence itself, how to make love as though your partner really is a sacred being passionately creating the Beginning of All Things with you, and how to know that the Earth is both your shelter and body and that all living things are your kin—blood of your blood. Mostly it is a book about living so well that your dying could be a shout of joy, rather than a desperate gasp for one more breath, because in your heart, you know that you missed out on the good stuff...the real stuff.

Gaia Eros is all about the real stuff. It just might bring you back to Life.

—Amber K
Priestess of Wicca
March 2004

Whatever you can do, or dream you can, begin it. Boldness
has genius, power, and magic in it.
—Goethe

Prologue

The eminent scientist Rene Dubos told us, "Our salvation depends upon our ability to create a religion of nature...suited to the needs and knowledge of modern humanity." What we are birthing is a truly planetary-Gaian-mythos that invites people of all traditions in our divided world to know themselves as children of the same Mother-Gaia Herself: Mother Earth.

But the creation and propagation of a myth requires more than scientific theories and technical papers. It requires a story, told not by academics, but sung by poets. Jesse Wolf Hardin has the soul and eloquence of a poet, and he has moved me to tears many times with his songs and stories—both recorded, as here, as well as told and sung in person. He is weaving the language for a Gaian mythos.

Anima Mundi

We have always known, in our deepest heart of hearts, that the Earth is alive. Throughout the world, even small children intuitively recognize Mother Earth. She is the oldest and most universally acknowledged religious archetype in all of human experience. Sculpted images of this primordial "Mother of all Mothers" date back at least to the Cro-Magnon Aurignacian peoples of 30,000 years ago, and are found across the Eurasian continent from Spain to Siberia. Indeed, as Wolf has pointed out, similar images have been found that push that dating back hundreds of thousands of years to Neanderthals and even *Homo erectus*. A crude prototype of the "Venus of Willendorf" was recently pulled from a 400,000-year-old deposit near the Moroccan city of Tan-Tan, carved from a piece of quartzite. Stone tools found in the same deposit were made by *Homo erectus*.

The idea that all life or all consciousness is interconnected is one of humanity's most enduring spiritual traditions; indeed, it is the very essence of what is called "The Perennial Philosophy." Human groups as various as the Iroquois, the Sufis, and the Western European Freemasons all incorporate it into their belief structures. References to it can be found in ancient documents of the classical world, both East and West. It is a compelling idea, spanning both millennia and the vast complexity of human cultures.

Carl Jung coined the term "collective unconsciousness" to refer to such a global mind; and Pierre Teilhard de Chardin described it as the Noosphere—a sheath of intelligence for the Earth, and the inevitable extension of the planetary biosphere. But the true heart of this understanding is found in the alchemical mystical concept of Anima Mundi—"The Spirit of the Earth." This term is nothing less than a Medieval rephrasing of the most ancient and primordial theological premise of "the Goddess" as Mother Earth, or Mother Nature. And it is the Spirit animating Jesse Wolf Hardin's lifetime of work.

Wolf and I have always shared a deep sense of the importance of land restoration and re-sacramentalization of sacred places as ways of returning to the Earth something of the great gifts that we receive from her. We embrace exactly the same perspective and understanding of Gaia and all her children, and I can think of few people with whom I find myself in such total agreement on every point. For decades, we have worked separately and together as allies and coconspirators in bringing Gaia into the forefront of modern human consciousness.

My Brother, Wolf

I first encountered Jesse Wolf Hardin in the mid-1970s through his inspired and inspiring essays and artwork—a powerful voice (and pen) bringing Paganism and a Gaian ethos into the radical environmentalist movement, helping to further the evolution of a contemporary land ethic. As an artist myself, I was particularly taken by his magickal shamanic drawings, in which intertwined forms of animals and people emerge from mystic landscapes like jungle vines. Wolf is credited with helping to bring the spirituality and environmental communities together, inspiring church congregations to get more active "for the Earth" while injecting a spiritual component into environmental groups, events, and publications. He has conveyed a deepened sense of environmental activism and Earth stewardship to the Pagan and New Age communities, where he has become a primary voice of deep ecology.

I finally got to meet Wolf in person in 1986, when he came to Ukiah, California, on a "Deep Ecology Medicine Show" concert tour, which I helped sponsor through the Church of All Worlds. As I listened to his songs and stories, I recognized a kindred spirit. In those days, he was known as Lone Wolf Circles, and I was known as Otter. As fellow animals, we sensed an immediate rapport. Wolf came to visit my lifemate, Morning Glory, and I at our home on the Rushing River, where he developed a relationship with my rehabilitating great horned owl, Archimedes.

Then in 1992, having resurrected *Green Egg* magazine after an 11-year hiatus, I recruited Wolf to write and illustrate a regular column called "Circling Home." I wanted all our readers to experience as much of his magic as we could fit into our pages. In June of 1996 I drew his portrait for the column header, which I present here in tribute. I think it captures the essence of this mystical canyon Shaman.

Wolf and I were both presenters at the the July 2002 Starwood Festival. We had not seen each other in six years and had a lot of catching up to do. We talked for many hours over several days, and I got to witness again his impassioned and spellbinding presentations to audiences. I was just in the process of putting together a proposal for New Page Books for *A Grimoire for the Apprentice Wizard*, and we discussed at great length the importance of providing a responsible mentorship for the next generation of Shamans and wizards now feeling "the Call." Out of these discussions grew the idea of convening the legendary "Grey Council" of mages and sages, wise ones, elders, and teachers. Beginning with the two of us, the Council soon grew to a couple dozen members, forming a review and advisory board of committed teachers to create a program of apprenticeship in Wizardry for the Grimoire. Throughout the project, Wolf was a major contributor, and the work is greatly enriched thereby.

My personal admiration for Wolf and his work is unbounded, and I look forward to the day when I go and quest in his sacred canyon. His Sanctuary is a place of power that brings alive for its guests "the sensuous and emotive spirit of Gaia," and their own personal gifts and callings.

The Awakening

We stand on the threshold of a New Age. After half a billion years of evolution, we have arrived at this magical moment. Gaia floats mighty yet vulnerably amidst the starry heavens. She calls to us, and touches our human hearts, and we know we are part of a self-aware mind capable of contemplating its own existence. And now, having seen herself through our satellite eyes, she is awakening to consciousness.

The Wheel is turning again, and the Goddess is reemerging. As in the ancient myths, Persephone is returning from the Underworld, to bask in the sunlight of a new dawn. She is beginning to awaken; her eyelids are fluttering. In her twilight sleep, her dreams are coming to life in us, and many, many of us are spontaneously hearing her call in our hearts. Just as the billions of neurons in our brains link up synergistically, so shall we participate in the awakening of Gaia herself—and our full apotheosis.

These are dark and troubled times. We who are attuned to the cycles of Nature and the rhythms of the Earth often feel overwhelmed by the escalating ecological and environmental crises. The atmosphere's ozone layer is compromised, global warming is dramatically changing our climate, and the destruction of the rainforests and the pollution of the seas are causing worldwide droughts. The challenges we face are so vast and the politics of greed and corruption so complex that it will truly take a miracle to transform such global destruction.

But miracles are what our magick is all about. Our hope and intention is that these writings will inspire others to join in this heroic mission of Earth Ministry, and that a new generation will feel the calling, and take up this path of service to all life, as champions of Gaia. Thus will our myths and magic manifest in reality in our daily lives, improving and blessing the world.

So Mote It Be!

—Oberon Zell-Ravenheart
September 21, 2003

Preface

Somewhere, as we speak, a Pagan affinity group is hard at work preparing the next Beltane ritual in its area. A circle of bearded priests gathers to revitalize the nearly lost sensibilities of ancient Druidry. An ecofeminist "locks down" with other activists to protest globalization and the environmental policies of the World Trade Organization (WTO). A dance troupe choreographs its interpretation of indulgent goddesses and wild canyons as a way of trying to educate and inspire the world. A man contacts self and planet more deeply through his artful preparation of wild foods and a woodstove-baked pie. A couple or threesome embrace Spirit, in the course of passionately and mindfully embracing each other. A clan or coven is pooling its resources to buy, restore, and resacrament a piece of land where its community can pilgrimage and gather. Having yet to find like-minded people in her neighborhood, a young woman in braids and a lacy dress begins her study of Wicca as a focused and determined solitaire.

In an age of accelerating distraction and advancing destruction, each makes his or her heroic journey in the direction of presence and place, authenticity and response-ability, reconnection and rewilding, sensation and celebration, clarity and power, assignment and purpose, tribe and truth. Taking risks, pushing the envelope, doing all they can to help. They are the small but growing number who refuse to numb down or look away, empathics who feel both the suffering and joy of the world in every cell of their being—seekers experiencing the world through reawakened primal instinct and their so called "sixth sense," through their caring hearts, through every inch of skin. And each draws insight and instruction from relationship with the living, inspirited Earth. They are the inheritors of, practitioners of, and living vehicles for what we call New Nature Spirituality (NNS).

Gaia Eros is a collection of essays and instructions for anyone interested in the various forms and practices falling under this umbrella. With my having abandoned school at an early age, these are hardly the words of an academic! They represent instead the lessons of hard-earned experience and manifest epiphany. They contain not conclusions so much as revelations: insights and tools revealed by a purpose-filled and caring land...and a particular stretch of enchanted forest canyon. The following chapters were composed on a solar powered Apple laptop, from a small desk overlooking a scene of mating heron and meandering river. Together they create a handbook for Earth-informed magical practice: inspiration to live every moment to the fullest...the means for identifying and the inspiration for fulfilling our personal, most meaningful purpose.

New Nature Spirituality incorporates or is resonant and allied with various aspects of ancient primal mind, Shamanism, Totemism, Animism, Paganism, Buddhism, Norse Cosmology, the Animism of Africa, the "Red Road" of Native America, Celtic Druidry, and archaic Wicca. And yet it is more than a reenactment or resurfacing of earlier traditions, more than a return to the "old ways." Included within are elements of contemporary theosophy, ecospirituality, ecofeminism, Unitarianism, communitarianism, creation spirituality, deep ecology, conservation biology, ecopsychology, and new science. We're not talking about an eclectic amalgam of favorite ideas, so much as directly accessing the same inspirited Source that has informed every magical practice throughout time: the living world, Gaia!

This new Earth-instructed paradigm addresses the spiritual needs and magical proclivities of seekers coming into their own both today and in the coming generations: folks of mixed blood and mixed heritage, those growing up inundated with secular cynicism and separative technology, and those facing social and environmental meltdown often with little affirmation from their family and little support from their society. It offers to give us back our most authentic selves, awareness of our magical powers, childlike wonder and delight. It provides a deepened sense of place to the uprooted (in a mental or mobile sense) and like-hearted community to the perpetually alone. It inspires us to listen to and follow the imploring of our hearts, even as our schools teach the superiority of the rational mind. While modernist thinking holds that all things are equally true and relevant, New Nature Spirituality brings us full circle to the responsibilities of discernment and choice...to meaning and mission. It contributes a plethora of gods and goddesses, the many faces of the One, intermediaries and spirits through which we come to know the absolute unity and inseparability of the living universe. And to the displaced and dissatisfied, to those who never quite "fit in" anywhere else, it offers a home.

New Nature Spirituality is the antithesis of denial: we practitioners don't deny truth, no matter how hard it is to hear. But neither do we deny our visions and needs, urges and hungers. In all its diverse manifestations, it becomes the personalized religion of sensualists and celebrants—reaping the rewards for awareness and engagement in the now, tasting every flavor, every nuance of what it means to be fully, completely alive. It is the religiosity of hot springs and back rubs, of "yums" and "ooohs" and "ahhs," of social experiment and ecoactivism, of untamed wilderness and mindful lovemaking. Of extended families, covens, and land-based tribes. It insists that regardless of what anyone else says, we are all born with some capacity to make magic...and that such magic can be directed towards making things more healthful, enjoyable, beautiful, and right.

Join with those who honor the power and lessons of the seasons, the ascendancy of a full moon, the transitioning of the sun. The sacredness of women and the blessings of manhood. Our native sexuality, and the power of intuition. The importance of integrity, and the urgency of response. Those who honor windswept mountain peaks and forests tall. The wisdom of creatures big and small.

You, too, are called.

Chapter 1

Magic and Mystery

*To Practice magic is to bear the responsibility for having a
vision.*

—Starhawk

*They gave him a seashell: "So you'll learn to love the water."
They opened a cage and let a bird go free: "So you'll learn to
love the air." They gave him a little bottle sealed up tight.
"Don't ever, ever open it. So you'll learn to love mystery."*

—Eduardo Galeano

It's a scene replayed over and over again throughout the history of human
kind: the shadows of a circle of elders tilting and gesturing like giants on the
faces of surrounding rock. Children more curious than obedient watch from
behind a concealing oak or jungle hedge, straining their ears to make out the
strange words and glorious sounds being carried starward aboard the roar of
a ceremonial fire. In every case, the elders would be Adepts, having both
trained for and survived the tests that prepare one to intercede with the
powers of Nature, or win favor with the gods and goddesses for a besieged or
hungering tribe. They first wore little but fate and feathers that decorated
taut black skin, then the furs of reindeer and cave bears, the horn headdresses
of Tuva and Lascaux. A gathering of Druid priests. Norse soothsayers. Apache
medicine men. The Aborigines of Australia. Greek Orphics. The Pythoness.
The priestesses of Aphrodite and Diana. Witnesses could only imagine the
secretive motions of hands concealed behind flowing purple robes or ashen
hooded cloaks—as the practitioners of every Nature-based society, at each
stage of history, performed their sacred rites. They mystify not only the wide-
eyed children, but those adults who have neither been selected for, nor yet
completed the special training required by any esoteric tradition. There is
indeed power in the focused attentions of the inner circle…and there is power
for all in the mystery of the unknown.

Magic is the venerable art of storing and manifesting that power, directing subtle energies in accordance with a vision or mission. It is the physics of

imagination and intent. Since the days of the Paleolithic Shaman, we've known that a combination of personal intention and will, rituals, and spells can by themselves influence the likelihood of a particular intended effect, result, or outcome.

Some are born more predisposed to such practice and calling, but everyone has a degree of ability to magically affect and alter events, and the power is amplified many-fold by those alliances of intention sometimes called covens, nests, or clans. Even without physical real-time participation, a common group vision can move human evolution in any direction, positive or negative. As with fire or any other energy, magic is in itself morally neutral. And because of this, it becomes incumbent on the magical traditions to dedicate their intention and skills to doing good: contributing clarity, defining priorities, serving the needs of the heart and the hopes of the children. Continually healing and binding the relationship between self and others, and between the people and the Earth. Giving thanks and praise for every lesson and gift. Guarding, restoring, sacramenting, and celebrating the actual places of power that provide us with inspiration and instruction.

While there are certainly cases of magic being used for evil, the majority of sorcerers are always "source-erers" who are pledged to the natural and spiritual Source, the mother of sustenance and imaginings. The word *magic* is derived from the Greek *magos*, meaning "wizard" or "wise one," and from the earlier Persian *magus*, meaning "royal magician-priests." These "Magi" were diviners, healers, and astrologers known to have honored the divinity of the entire living cosmos, and the sacred haoma (soma) they drank likely included psychedelic mushrooms that helped reveal the intricacies of the magical universe. The Celtic Druids protected the sacred oak groves where they gathered. Native American practitioners bless the modes of human perception and human activity that contribute to the health of the land, creating taboos and curses to limit any behavior that could damage the ecosystem, denigrate the holy, or demean the spirits. Respect for God (gods or goddesses) has meant respect for creation and the creative force—Mother Earth, Pachamama, Assaya, Prithivi, Gaia. The natural world was seen as an embodiment of Spirit, and the place one goes in order to glean the wishes, insights, and suggestions of the sacred Whole. The veneration of a pre-Christian horned god was no precursor to satanism or devil worship, but rather, the affirmation of the noble wild within us all, the ways in which the magical human combines the strength of the stag, the inner-sight of the owl, and the loyalty and insistence of the wolf.

An intentional change in consciousness is magical in its own right, it's true. But the greatest magic may be the ways we focus and extend out that consciousness in order to actively influence the world for the better. It is this most selfless manifestation that, in the long run, empowers, validates, and fulfills the magical self. There are able individuals who can and do direct energy in order to win romantic dates, cast a spell for financial success, or even ensure a parking place at work...but the most intense magic—the greatest miracles—occur when we're aligned with and collaborate with natural and native forces, with ongoing evolutionary processes, and with the intent and will of the self-directed Earth.

And so it has often been. Alchemy was more about the mutability of natural elements and the transformational processes of consciousness than it was the transmutation of lead into gold (although that possibility undoubtedly earned the alchemist more benefactors than the rewards of personal growth and change). Animism was not only the recognition of disembodied spirits, but the knowledge that all things in Nature are imbued with Spirit. Wicca is an Earth-honoring practice informed by the grounded wisdom of healers and midwives, land stewards and agents of love. A megalith is not only a reminder of the power of the Earth, but it is Earth's spokesperson, a spokesrock. Clairvoyance, the ability to discern that which is beyond the immediate senses, exists because we are connected at greater energetic levels to all that is and all that has ever been. Divination is the knowledge of unfolding events, provided by a more intense than normal understanding of the past and engagement with the present. The tarot deck doesn't foretell fortunes so much as clarify patterns and potentials, for what every magician knows is always the decisive moment. A talisman connects us to the natural sources of information and power. Portents and omens are easy to interpret when we are conscious of our cellular relationship with the natural world. Such practices and powers are not supernatural or beyond Nature, but intranatural, intrasensible—of, by, and for the magical world of which Nature is an essential component.

In the vernacular of modern society, *magic* is often poorly defined as synonymous with "illusion" and "chicanery." And indeed, there has always been an element of showmanship and trickery to the practice of magic. But while prestidigitation, pyrotechnics, and the power of suggestion have long been used by magicians as part of their art, it's generally been to alert and enlist rather than to awe or manipulate. These kinds of perception-altering skills can wrest the audience's attention away from assumption and habit, provoking a suspension of disbelief, opening eyes to the less obvious and more complex processes and manifestations of real, employable magic. There's nothing quite like a sudden explosion of sparks or a voice from the beyond to grab people's attention. Then once they're fully in "attendance," every manner of enchantment, every act of magic becomes possible.

Similarly, technological gadgetry may be inscrutable and even amazing, but it is not magic. Video, holographic projections, and biofeedback machines are readily employed by modern wizards to arrest the certainty and doubt of the people they work with, making them more susceptible to the true magical processes. Real magic cannot be adequately verified, quantified, or qualified by any present or future scientific means. And it can be neither controlled nor harnessed, reduced nor replicated. It is always that which lies just beyond the understandings and manipulations of the scientific paradigm. Magic itself remains invisible, though we are often both instrumental to its success and witness to its effects.

We hear different magical and philosophic traditions referred to as "Mystery Schools." This is because they each honor the power of the mysterious, not because their rites are withheld or their rituals beyond our understanding. They are schools of belief that embrace the "mysterium," the combined forces of Spirit and Nature that one comes to know through intimacy and intercourse rather than reasoning and comprehension. Magic is the application of the uncanny and the unlikely in the service of transformation—our own. And with our personal realization comes the opportunity to fulfill our most meaningful purpose: to honor the needs of the Earth and the will of Spirit.

The ceremonial fires die down sometime between the setting of the moon and the rise of a new day's sun. One by one, the hooded figures make their way from the circle and down the darkened trail toward the sea. The children have long ago returned to their straw-filled beds, all except perhaps a single young man or woman determined at all costs to learn the Adepts' fateful practice. From the ranks of the insistent few a new generation ever rises to take the baton, the walking stick, the magic wand. The root and reason for their power is Gaia, they know...and that from the fertile soils of mystery, all magic flows.

*Remember your story, our story. Clothe yourself in your
authority. You speak not only as yourself or for yourself. You
were not born yesterday. You have been through many dyings
and know in your heartbeat and bones the precarious,
exquisite balance of life. Out of that knowledge you can speak
and act. You will speak and act with the courage and
endurance that has been yours through the long, beautiful
aeons of your life story as Gaia.*

—Joanna Macy

Some introductory questions:

- Before this pivotal juncture of rebecoming, just who did you think you were?

- What were your expectations for yourself?

- What were the expectations others had for you?

- What failings did you imagine you have? Which did you deny?

- What reassuring illusions did you cultivate?

- What fears fostered and fed your illusions?

- Who are you now, apart from who you thought you were, who your parents, friends, and lovers wanted you to be, and what society expects of you? Who are you apart from your rejection of and resistance to such people and expectations?

- What were your earliest connections to Nature? When did you start disconnecting from its will and example, and what brought you back into her lap?

- What magical events have happened in your life, and what magical powers have you discovered in yourself?

- What are the messages and implications of such magic? How can you manifest and direct this magic for the good of the inspirited Whole?

- What is the difference between obligation and responsibility?

- To what are you responsible, and in what order of priority?

- In what ways can sexual energy and identity both contribute to and distract from sacred purpose and wholeness?

- Intimacy is easily confused with sexuality. What stands in the way of true intimacy with self, others, and Earth?

- Meditate on what it means to be truly "grounded."

- All wise cultures have been place based, and place informed—meaning an outgrowth and extension of a particular ecosystem and watershed. Think of what you can do to develop a similar reciprocal relationship with a particular region, mountain, or river?

- Nature is one big gifting cycle. What are the gifts you were born with or came by naturally, and what are the most powerful and beautiful ways you can manifest and share them?

- What are the most wonderful, meaningful, and effective gifts you can give to yourself? To others? To a mission? To the land? To future generations of life?

- What gifts have you been given by others, and what additional gifts are you willing to accept...and accept that you deserve?

- What were your childhood visions and dreams? In what ways have or haven't you lived them out?

- What are the differences between desires and needs?

- What are the real needs and desires of your inner child-self?

- What acts express, affirm, deepen, expand, validate, and fulfill your essential inner self?

- What acts compromise, assuage, distract, devalue, dilute, or dishonor that self?

- What sorts things are you upset about, and what keeps you from expressing your anger?

- The pace of activity of even the most essential and wonder-full missions can still prevent us from slowing down enough to fully be, and thereby know. Describe your being, apart from your doing.

- Intellection impinges on sensation, intuition, and instinct. What do you feel in the precious silence between thoughts?

- In what ways have future considerations robbed from the present?

- In what ways have intellection and busy-ness diverted from problematic sentience, empathy, pain, intuition, and foresight?

- To what people, self-concepts, ideas, plans, and agendum are you attached? Which attachments contribute to the realization of self, Earth, and purpose? And which distract or obstruct?

- If you knew these were to be the final days of your life, what would you demand of them and yourself? What is to be felt and done? How do you want to be?

- Meditate on the difference between symptomatic happiness and fulfillment/contentment.

- What can you envision as your most natural, satisfying, and destiny-filled future? What home, what friends, what alliances, what assignments?

- Your work begins with a great surrendering, and emptying of the pure vessel. How can you best tend to the needs, contribute to the growth, nurture the dreams, and fulfill the purpose of that essential flawless core that remains?

- Make an evolving list of irrevocable commitments you can begin making to your deserving self, others, projects, Earth, and Spirit.

- What are the most present, focused, artful, meaningful, effective, soul-filled, magical, generous, and gracious ways of fulfilling and honoring those commitments?

- For what would you be willing to risk your life?

- For what purpose or end are you willing to be at all times fully, responsibly, excruciatingly alive?

- Gaia, the inspirited Earth, is trying to get your attention, trying to communicate and commune with you. Without using any words, describe for yourself what it means to really listen.

Chapter 3

The Song of Gaia:
The Living Earth as Source and Mentor

*We must not expect that we can simply use the...image of Gaia
to meet emotional, religious (or) political needs without
allowing it to transform us in unexpected and radical ways.
The spirituality of the Earth is...an invitation to initiation, to
the death of what we have been and the birth of something new.*

—David Spangler

It was said that in the beginning nothing existed but the Great Mother, Chaos—a dark swirling of the elements in a vast cauldron of time. Atomic matter spun about wildly in a mad dance of self-absorption, as spiraling gases mixed and stirred within her being. It was said that from the disorder of this tempestuous womb, a child of order was born, cast at an ideal temperature at the perfect distance from the sun, a body, heart, and soul spun into a globe of minerals and chemicals, land and sea, fur and feathers, tears and laughter. They spoke of it as a living entity manifest in intricate patterns that constantly rearranged themselves in service to the Whole, a breathing planet delivered into the black sands of a cosmic desert.

The ancient Greeks proclaimed this geobiological composite a goddess, and named this goddess "Gaia." In Piraeus, Dodona, and Delphi they built beautiful marble temples to honor her—the source of life, wisdom, and thus of joy—places where she spoke to and through those oracles able and willing to make out her whispered guidance. Plato described the Earth as "a living creature, one and visible, containing within itself all living creatures," and according to Xenophon, teaching "justice to those who can learn." "The better she is served," he counsels, "the more good things she gives in return." Here is a relationship worthy of Homeric verse:

To Gaea, mother of all life and oldest of gods, I sing. You who make
and feed and guide all creatures of the Earth, those who move on your
firm and radiant land, those who wing your skies and swim your seas,
all those you've given birth Mistress, from you come all our harvests,
our children, our night of day. To you who contain everything, to Gaea
mother of all, I sing.

Those people living closest to the land have always placed the Earth deity foremost in their system of worship. It's easier to accept the primacy of an inspirited Earth when it's directly providing one with all the things needed for a healthy and aesthetic life. Yet as late as the 17th century, these essential truths continued to surface:

> *The whole world is knit and bound within itself: for the world*
> *is a living creature, everywhere both male and female, and the*
> *parts of it do couple together...by reason of their mutual love.*
>
> —Della Porta, 1658

This understanding survived the ascension of the sky gods and the new soteriological (salvational) religions, persisted even as humanity clustered more and more in its swelling cities, and receded only after the last of our connections to the land had been severed by the shears of scientism in the "age of reason." Ideas are trivialized that betray the dominant system, while those ideas that serve its bent are encouraged and, in time, institutionalized. The model of the world that worked best for the merchants and corporations, the developers and colonizers, was no longer that of a living being requiring our respect and forbearance. The new model was one of a planet machine with gears and pulleys—a giant watch awaiting our enlightened improvements. The emotional, intuitive, instinctual self was increasingly discouraged in favor of the rational, the functional, and the quantifiable. The tribal dances largely gave way to marches, and the songs were forgotten.

While the Greeks abandoned their mythology of an Earth goddess long ago, it is by the name they gave her that the symbol of "Earth Mother" has reemerged in contemporary consciousness. This universal symbol has been powerfully revived thanks to Oberon Zell-Ravenheart's 1970 paper "TheaGenesis: Birth Of A Goddess" and the subsequent writings of NASA researchers James Lovelock and Lynn Margulis, whose "Gaia Hypothesis" postulates a self-regulating and intentional living planet. In a synergy of the scientific and the metaphysical, we find an increased recognition of the Goddess just as humanity seems to need the wisdom and alliance of the Earth the most. In 1985, a refreshing new conference asked the question: "Is the Earth a living organism?" committing what heretofore had been considered scientific blasphemy, while inquiring about something taken for granted by most indigenous peoples. To our "primitive" ancestors, intimate with the energies and physique of the planet, the Earth was almost universally experienced as a sacred living being and as their extension, source, and destination.

Scientists trained to focus exclusively on the parts, advised to specialize in a narrow field such as industrial chemistry or molecular biology, can hardly be faulted for a failure to envision the incorruptibility of an interactive whole. However informed they might be, professionals find themselves at a distinct disadvantage next to the broad vision of Earth-based peoples and the open minds of children. The sciences have narrowed their focus a bit like a flea, and while well versed on the nutritional offerings of a stretch of skin, they are likely oblivious to the overall form and function of the animal that bears them. The disappearance of general physicians able to diagnose and treat the entire patient is an analogy for this specialization of the sciences. No expert in one area is likely to be proficient in the other important studies, and few have opportunities for the cross-disciplinary experience necessary for a subsequent understanding of the symbiotic Whole.

Lovelock called the Earth's regulatory self-controls, including both temperature and the composition of the atmosphere, "the song of life." We participate by co-creating the very air we breathe, in alliance with the volcanoes and microbes, the various plants, and our fellow aspiring and perspiring animals. We might think of each individual being as a cell, grouped with others into cohesive organs of the planet body, each with specific innate functions that contribute to the overall balance and health of the Whole. When speaking of the human body, such a condition of collaborative balance would be called "homeostasis." In the language of song, we refer to this interactive condition as multipart harmony, with all the performers delivering their diverse individual parts in key, and in perfect pitch with the rest. In our spiritual vernacular, we call this state "resonance." It's interesting that Lovelock's conjecturing began with his contemplation of atmosphere, the "breath of God." The air's suspended molecules form the connective tissue, the bridge between our bodies and the trees behind us, the buildings ahead and those clouds floating languorously above. The song is the collected vibrations of every Gaian form and process, transported across a membranous transparency, carried through the air to every willing ear.

Because of the collaborative nature of this song, it could be said that we work in concert to maintain the composition of life—life orchestrated by a unifying presence, performed by a wide range of inspirited constituents with complimentary instrumentation. Lovelock himself saw no clear distinction between the proactive performers—rocks and whales, life and "nonlife"— "merely a hierarchy of intensity." What he was describing was a scientifically posited reality previously expressed solely as a religious idea.

The Earth has developed systems that somehow recharge each other in the process of interaction, reacting and exchanging elements with no overall loss. In a natural state of balance, living beings actively give back to the Whole, equal to what they take, managing to consume their environment without degrading it. Gaia forms a single system that miraculously recycles its resources without quantitatively or qualitatively depleting its parts. While it lives off the sun, the sun doesn't run down any faster as a result of the Earth utilizing more of its available energy. Gaia has set an example of nonexploitive partnership, an example for the planets of distant galaxies, and an example for us as well.

To the ancient Greeks, we were both blessed and cursed with the unique ability to self-reflect, and thus to imagine ourselves distinctly apart from the rest. The great oral tragedies told of the anguish of recognizing the importance of our individual assignments, coupled with a particularly human awareness of our impending mortal demise. The key to inner peace was always in aligning oneself with the will of Gaia, adapting to her patterns, tapping her prevalent energetic momentum in the accomplishment of selfhood, the fulfillment of role. To this end, they regularly sought out divine guidance. Not "divine" as in other-worldly, but as in "divined"—derived from the greater, larger self, channeled directly from the inspirited planet holon. Those accepting of the living Earth have always moved close to it to hear the Shamans of Tuva throat-singing on the dirt floors, AmerIndians vision-questing in dug-out pits, and the early Irish opening to signs inside the "Tigh'n alluis," the Celtic sweat lodge. Believing in Gaia, whether as a working mechanical model or as an inspirited being, it nonetheless becomes increasingly difficult to recognize her needs and communications as we tend to live further insulated from the land and the elements, further from the unobstructed Gaian presence we call "nature" or "wilderness." The most valid impressions of the workings of Gaia are more likely to result from personal intimacy with the flesh of her being than from clever extrapolation. Our role within this Whole is clarified not by taking charge, but by adjusting to its organic tendencies, and by directly sensing the extant will of the planet organism.

Gaian consciousness is likely a synesthetic process in which it synthesizes the perceptive field of all its constituent beings. Consider the Earth made conscious through the combined complimentary perception of its parts, through the eyes of the hawk, the responses of plant life, the comprehension of deer, the sensation of fruit in a desert tortoise's mouth, and the burgeoning hearts of children. I believe Gaia knows the galaxy through the dreams of its seekers, the magnetic-field sensitivity of migrating mallards, the holophonic echolation of whales, the wind-tugged strands of spiderwebs and the probing fingers of the blind: Gaian "body language." If this exchange of information were between unconnected entities, we would call it "communication," but because it occurs between constituent elements of a connective Whole, it is more a matter of "communion"—an open, simultaneous, wordless sharing with our living context, with the rest of the inclusive All. Communion is the immediate awareness of our immersion, while the rest of the time our subconscious body continues its exchange with the world minus any conscious acknowledgement. An awakening to the full experience is inevitably blissful and transformative, the state of self-realization and intense mindfulness also known as satori, samadhi, or enlightenment. It's about reentering the depths of Gaian reality, deep seeing, tasting, smelling, dreaming, touching, and shaping the world that is us. A fully informed world.

We know the instruction and will of the inspirited universe through the deep empathic experiencing of Gaia, and we access the truth and experience of Gaia through the portals of the feeling heart. It thus appears we do ourselves as well as our evolving communities a disservice if we merely substitute a goddess Gaia for the more conventional, omnipotent sky god in our metaphysical pantheon. She is not some removed authority or elevated reference point, but the fact of and means for our sacred oneness. She is inseparable from the miraculous Whole, as we are inseparable from the song and miracle of her.

For all the readings of his sensitive instruments, Lovelock may have come closest to capturing the essence of Gaia when he spoke of that "song" of life. With the destruction of life form and terraform, there's a loss of communicants. Notes are missed, then whole stanzas vanish forever from the summer winds, and from the curling faded page. Devoted to its modality, the value of its parts and the integrity of its composition, Gaia responds by innovating substituting passages—extending the bridge between codependent parts, speeding up or slowing down the tempo as necessary, drawing on the strengths of the remaining parts to fill out the texture of the Whole. It is the Whole that decides when our pitch is too sharp or too flat, and it is up to us to spot the key and meter signs, the signature that marks our entry into the piece in progress, our place in the arrangement.

The opus surrounds us, beckoning us to participate. Encouragement abounds...in the acoustics of our bioregion, the overture of thunder, the rain's riffs and licks, the bagatelles of the arroyos' short-lived floods, the ocean waves' tireless refrain. In the fugue of mating frogs, the counterpoints of shore birds, the ravens' stuttering arpeggios, and the suite of wind-whipped pines. Each earthen entity responds from its own being, to the directives of its form, its place, its purpose: the soil slow, adagio, and the granite peaks adagissimo. The mourning doves, funerale. Delicato, little ladybugs. The soft flowers, sotto voce. Fiero, bold elk, challenging fellow suitors, whistling for your mate. Furioso, uncaged fire. Comedic coyote, burlesco, if you please. The bear, the volcano, fortissimo, hombres. And the people, when they must talk, make it important, make it poetic, parlato. And as long as you're at it, why not make the delivery as sweetly as you can: dolce, dolce? From the dawn's glorious fanfare to the sunset's climactic coda, from life's bold opening to its decrescendo and finale, we ultimately have no choice but to proceed from one movement to the next.

In time, we as a species, or at least we as individuals may be able to tell when our mortal expression lives up to that organic, inherited consonance. Like the Earth herself, we endeavor to find our perfect rhythms. To express ourselves in the key of life. To discover and enjoin the holy grail of song...the sacred song of Gaia.

Chapter 4

Presence: Reclaiming the Sacred Now

A tragic sense of life...doesn't force us into a closed somber cone of depression and futility; it urges the opposite. The tragic sense opens a human being to the exuberant joys of the present. To laughter, carnality, the comical varieties of love, to music and art, to the small glories of the day.

—Peter Hamill

In H.G. Wells's classic *The Time Machine*, an adventurous researcher departs from his basement workshop in a futuristic vehicle of his own making, leaving nothing behind but a circular impression in the dust where it once stood. In the same way, we "civilized" people are often out of touch, absent, unreachable by a world of unfolding presence. Our bodies linger in place much like that impression in the dust, while our minds orbit backward and forward through the years and the centuries, inhabiting every place but here...and every period of time but now.

All the while, the rest of contiguous creation are reaching out to us, seeking to regain contact and redevelop relationship, offering to inspire, nourish, and inform their estranged hominid brethren. These exchanges are at once energetic, physical, and spiritual, and only as deep as our presence. Whether revering, consuming, or celebrating another, all exchanges, all relationships benefit to the degree that we are wholly in body, in place, in momentous present time.

This is just as true whether we live in suburban, rural, or urban environments, and no matter where on this Earth we call home. Indeed, the loss of presence results not only in a decrease in the intensity of our lived experience, but in the loss of clean air and open space. What appears to be good-natured tolerance of bright lights and loud sirens, social inequality, and a degrading environment...is often a lack of presence on our part. It fosters neglect of our crucial connection to self, Earth, and Spirit, and bolsters the preoccupation and intellection that makes both mass extinctions and disappearing forests possible. Social, psychological, and ecological imbalance grow out of our imagined separation from the natural world. And such imaginings can only occur in the abstract, beyond the influence of place, outside of present time. Nuclear war, acid rain, the abuse of children, occur in part because of our tendency to "dwell on" our hopes and worries, rather than dwelling *in* the moment, *in* place. It is in the present that injustice is most intolerable, and beauty most sweet.

When folks make the long trip to our Earthen Spirituality Project and Sweet Medicine Women's Center, an enchanted wildlands sanctuary, one of the first things we do is have them take off their watches. Everything in Nature is rhythmic and timely, and yet nothing is "on time." No hawk sightings, epiphanies, or orgasms happen at some predetermined hour, and the most significant and meaningful events are never marked on the day-planner— they surprise us, arriving just in time but never on schedule. On more than one occasion, in fact, visitors' watches have simply and inexplicable stopped. It's a mystery that we attribute to the power of this ancient ceremonial site...and to the absolute necessity of escaping from the paradigm of months and seconds, back into real time, real world, before any hopeful change can take place.

The now can never fit into a schedule, for it is both too big and too fleeting for that. Mark the now on your mental list, and it is already gone. The calendar we focus on describes a world that isn't here, which as any child would tell us, pales in comparison to that which is!

The experiencing of present time is, indeed, a *present*—a gift—from life, from Spirit, to us. A gift we pay a high price for ignoring. Both usages of *present* originate in the Latin adjective *praeséns*, meaning "at hand, now, here." The gift at hand, close enough to touch.

If it's disrespectful to turn down a gift—to turn one's back on a speaker or preacher in the midst of making his point—then surely it is all the more so to ignore the miracle of the moment, to turn away from the present experience and face inward toward some mind-bound movie. To ignore the communications of the world around us and focus in on our own internal dialogue. Or to pass by the awakening dandelion, absorbed by a mental picture of a wrapped rose at some distant florist. We get literally "caught up" with abstract thought, caught and held fast like fish in a trawler's net, surrounded on all sides by wide-eyed images and flailing priorities. Caught up in our heads, while the vital world our minds hope to describe passes below us as we walk, and sits up and watches us while we dream at night. All the while reality waves its arms and wings and cloud forms like flags trying to win back our attention.

Every moment is a *decisive* moment, a choice between fixating on our mental storehouse of images, or looking out the window at the birds looping through the sky. A choice repeated over and over again every minute of the day, with both attendant benefits and a high price to pay either way. With increased awareness, one may no longer be able to turn away from the fateful play of the moment, no matter how agonizing the scene might be. If we are to truly inhabit present time, we'll hear the cries of the helpless as we walk the streets, unable to drown them out with thoughts about the job we're walking home from, a litany of schedule and finance, a repeat of the last song we heard on the workplace radio. The sounds of the traffic may not be pleasant, but we will acknowledge each whir and grind that go to make it up, like any awakened animal would. We'll find no way to ignore the odors from the alleyway, nor block out the cold feel of a winter wind on our cheeks with pictures of the warm room awaiting us.

No perfume is lost to the unguarded nose, and that which bravely acknowledges the smells of the gutter surely feasts on a walk through the garden, truly delights in the olfactory playground of a lover's heated neck. Before the word "dwell" came to mean "to inhabit," it meant "to linger." Thus when eating, we may find our consciousness dwells within a world of taste, as our being lingers inside the flavor of each special moment. For a circle of drummers, the reward for being "on time" is an experiential rhythmic bonding, an entraining that ushers in a heightened condition of awakeness. The same for us. Sensing and reacting to the unfolding world "on time," in present time, we're rewarded with the passion and awe common to our fellow creatures, engorged in a state of arousal and response.

Too often, though, we find ourselves reading or listening to the news while we eat, the rich combinations of food stimulating the receptors in our mouths experienced only peripherally while the hungry body goes on "automatic pilot." Our conscious mind travels into other times, missing those flavors that entertain the present. Except for the first bite, we may consume an entire meal barely paying attention to its banquet of sensation, the fine distinctions between spoonfuls of the same entrée, the slow sensuous melt of butter fats, the interplay of heady spices. What could be more of a loss, more disrespectful of the giver, then failing to fully taste what's in our mouths, to give less than our complete attention to the fingers of the masseuse kneading our backs, or to picture past affairs while being tended by our lover today? To pine away at the loss of the sunset, while even now the glory of a new dawn stretches out before us?

Of course, even if we fight to avoid the vivid awareness and troubling responsibilities of the present, we're likely thrust back into the moment with the first clap of thunder, the nearby strike of lightning, a violent threat, or screeching tires approaching in the direction of the sidewalk we're moving along! And for those us of willing to make this reclamation conscious and purposeful, there are aids as well.

Recess may be the key. We need to recess class, recess Logos, recess our obsession with what has yet to come as well as what happened before. No matter what its title, the last course one attended is always "history." The historical epoch that stretches all the way back through time, begins in that very microsecond that just passed! In recess the present takes over, the child in us pulled out of intellection by the challenge and physicality of the monkey bars, the teasing climbable branches of trees in the yard, the random stimulation of so many other glad, spinning youths. Screams and laughter vanquish the ghost-like echoes of contemplation and the furies of future and worry. Here are grass smells and primal needs that reclaim them, an orgy of truly living color that grabs their attention back from the black-and-white movies projected in the theaters of their minds. Abstraction is defeated by children, activists, and dreamers...in the experiential, sensual swirl of recess!

Recess is a return—not to our nostalgic past, but to the swinging, playing, hurting, loving now. We're returned with the first tart bite of an orange, a morning's splash of cold water on our face, a sudden starting or stopping of the evening wind, the first glimpse of a falcon dropping through the air in pursuit of downtown pigeons. We're returned by the whiff of homemade bread, fresh out of the oven, the demanding ministrations of massage, and the magic of a sparrow feeding its babies in a hollow street sign. In reentering the present, in reentering the flesh of the realized moment, we are then ourselves penetrated...by every real thing around us, by the weather and the ground, by the people that are with us, by the totality of life.

Only in the now can we hope to be sufficiently conscious of place to sense our belonging to it, or to heed its will. In reinhabiting the present, all time becomes "home-time," and we're welcomed back no matter how often we try to leave it. Welcomed here, in place. Welcomed in the now...and in this way, welcomed home.

Chapter 5

Coming to Our Senses

*You must concentrate yourself and consecrate yourself wholly
to each day, as though a fire were raging in your hair.*

—Deshimaru

Our physical and intuitive senses are tools for this reinhabitation—
connecting us in a real way to the rest of this feeling world, to increased
response-ability...and to the immediate rewards of taste and touch,
sensation and bliss.

In New Nature Spirituality, we know that we live in order to *feel*—and
feel in order to praise and celebrate that life. We sense and relate to the
world through the complex symbiosis of emotion and instinct we call the heart,
through the "five senses," and those unmeasured faculties such as intuition
and precognition that scientists have lumped together as the "sixth sense."
While one can benefit by learning the "facts" about any chosen bioregion or
terrain, we can never really know a place by reading a book on the subject or
by thinking about it. We only come to know it like a baby, humbly and
appreciatively touching and tasting the world we're a physical, integral part
of—launched bodily into the experience and knowledge of place: the eyes
seeing every nuance of undressed life, sucking its hitchhiking molecules up
through the passages of the anxious nose. Reading the vibrations in the air as
they play across the taut tissues of our eardrums. Trying like that baby to put
the entire world into our mouths, constantly reaching out to handle it. Our
natural response to our being born is to pull the substance and meaning of
the world closer to us, or by grabbing a hold, to pull ourselves ever closer to
it. In this way life "makes sense," and our senses make the experience of life.

The practices of New Nature Spirituality are antidotes to the cognitive
disassociation of modern human kind. Ritual and magic reconnect us to our
bodies and the body of inspirited Gaia. Mindfulness is a component of both
awareness and sacrament. Social and environmental activism puts us "in
touch" with what matters most. The act of restoring wild places (wildcrafting)

feeds us like nothing else. And wildcrafting can be a port of reentry to the experience and purpose of self and place. We learn cordage—fashioning raw plant fiber into rope—not because we expect to find ourselves lost in the wilderness, but because we know it will help us find ourselves again. And because of the way it binds us to our essential native selves, weaving us back into the fabric of Nature. We practice to avoid the slide into rote, habitual behavior, to prevent the dulling of the animal senses that connect us to the so-real world.

We can practice awareness wherever we are, and not just out in Nature. One can "stay awake" by noticing the way a chair cradles the back, the tickley way in which air dries the sweat on our neck, or the messages of hormonal pheromones released by others in the room. Each has something to impart to us, communicating through its energy, presence, and example the factors relevant to our being. Things such as the gift of wild foods growing at our feet, the fact that our neck may be sore if we don't change positions, that the window needs to be opened, or that somebody we love is very angry with us! Staying in-body and in-focus is a constant and unrelenting task, a challenge to willingly face the cauldron of tests, the bursting moment, the shadowless crucible. But one must actually *choose* to see less, hear less, feel less. We are individually responsible for our failures to perceive, and for what happens or doesn't happen when we've deliberately turned away. And likewise, we can take credit whenever we make the decision to wholly feel instead!

By looking, listening, smelling—we are touching, acknowledging, engaging, and thus affecting the world of which we're a part. Regardless of the degree to which we affect it, regardless of measurable results, we're nonetheless rewarded, immediately, for any "return to our senses": The ears that discern each element of discordant traffic are bestowed with the songs of the birds in every trimmed shrub. The nose that is trained to remain alert even in the presence of noxious fumes has a field day in line at the bakery. The eyes that meet the eyes of the world, behold the magic of unveiled truth. The hands that reach out are grasped in return.

The human body is an ecstatic organ, an agent and organ of Gaian bliss. The practice of its reinhabitation involves refamiliarizing ourselves with the feel and function of our flesh. We can start by attending the feel of our blood pushing through our veins, then the vibrations of the ground below us, then the point where our trembling rhythms intermesh with those of the Earth. Then, without moving from where you are, like an enthusiastic cook, isolate the ingredients of your experiencing, segregating and recombining each of the senses. With the eyes closed and ears plugged, know the world through the wind and whatever else touches you. Try to taste with the nose plugged.

Smell with the eyes closed, and try to identify each distinct aroma in the air, then attempt to triangulate your position in this way. With the eyes and nose blocked, try to measure and qualify the source of each sound occurring around you. In the woods or in a safe part of a park, plug all the head-bound senses and feel your way through the grass, examining every object with deft finger-tips alone, enjoying and communicating with the most ordinary of them as if they were remarkably new and unique to you, communing in the giving and receiving of touch.

By choosing to open up and pay attention, in time, we begin to notice the way different foods affect our energy levels, recognize the gentle effects of different herbs, and know the position of the moon without looking. We notice which postures cause us to tighten up and which increase our range of movement. Too much of our disappearing moments are spent drifting through inner space, the cerebral abyss. For our reprieve, we can thank any and all sources of "wake-up calls." Reprieval, and *retrieval.*

And why deprive ourselves, why diminish the depth and richness of a single lived moment? It really is a sensuous world we work, play, and dance through, a glad explosion of color and form! To know our place in such a world, to come home...we must first "come to our senses."

Come to them, I suggest, as we once left them behind.

Chapter 6

Sacred Indulgence:
Pleasuring Self and Other

Mysticism and exaggeration go together. A mystic must not fear ridicule if he is to push all the way to the limits of humility or the limits of delight.

—Milan Kundera

Properly loving each other—and loving this Earth—may begin with deeply loving and tending our own beings and bodies.

When people write Loba and me about their experiences here at the Earthen Spirituality Project, they may or may not mention the power of these Gaian insights or the impact of my counsel...but they seldom fail to thank us for the food they ate and the attention they got. To the extent that any teaching is cloaked in words, it can't be expected to make as much of an impression on us as those naked communications and revelations garnered through the five awakened senses. The talks I give suggest the importance of fully tasting the passing moments of our lives, while Loba's meals fairly demand it: "Pay attention!" cry the sweet-and-sour stir-fry, the homemade chili, and creamy sweet potato pie. No treatise can compare to the evocative gestures of a juniper limb, to the living text of mountains and rivers, or the murmuring and cooing of the canyon wind. I may wax eloquently about sensuality and bliss, but sometimes more is imparted by a single touch, a warm hug, or tender kiss.

It would be easy to pass this off as a human tendency to avoid deep spiritual or existential questions. Indeed, pleasure is often reduced to the level of vicarious, objectively experienced "entertainment" that distracts us from the immediacy of our personal feelings, needs, and dramas. On the other hand, indulging in deep conscious pleasure assists our reinhabitation of our sensate bodies, our communities, and the land we live in and on. Like pain, pleasure can function as a delivery system, catapulting us into the vital present moment and all it contains. Rather than isolating us, it dissolves boundaries, and heightens our sensual, visceral, and emotional connection to the Whole.

Furthermore, because it requires a degree of self-love, opening up to pleasure can help mend any schism between the spiritual and the physical, ease our fear of our bodily needs, and end the self-criticizing of our bodily forms. We have to accept that we are worthy, in a sense, in order to really give pleasure to ourselves, or to unselfconsciously accept pleasure from the people and places around us. We treat other people, and the living environment so much better once we've done the practical magic of properly treating ourselves, or of letting others treat us really, really well! It's far less likely someone will hurt another or wage war, overpopulate or overcompensate, become a drug addict or alcoholic, cut down the last old growth forests or neglect their spouse when they've learned to truly notice, tend, and honor their sacred selves. Their sacred bodies. Their holy mortal days. In this way, our indulging in pleasure is not only a means of feeling, but of dealing...and healing.

Indulgence is neither tolerance, license, nor excess. The word literally means to "satisfy one's innate hungers," and to "allow oneself to follow one's will." Society teaches us not to trust our feelings, and indulgence is our response: listening to our bodily desires and needs, the pleadings of intuition and instinct, and our heart's fateful call. Indulgence is a high-dive into the intimacy of sensation, pulling the universe closer so we can touch and taste it. It is manifest in a baby's wanting to put everything in its mouth, to taste, test, and perhaps savor. It is our acting out of the will and wisdom of the ancient knowing beings within us. It's both connection and reward—not only eating what's good for us, but eating meals that taste good.

Indulgence isn't about quantity. People may have sex with dozens of partners without truly indulging in the grace of each. Many consume quantities of food in an attempt to fill an emotional emptiness, or substitute for the nuances of flavors, smells, temperatures, and textures they fail to notice. True indulgence requires rolling the food around on our tongue, eating our toast butter-side down and giving its oils time to saturate the taste buds before commencing to chew. Eating slower and more attentively, the indulgent diner actually consumes less than the inattentive, and the indulgent lover is more intensely focused than libertine.

As with sexuality, pampering the body can be either sacred or profane depending on the energy and intention we put into it. We can make either of these a sacrament by focusing on our connection to the sacred Whole, recognizing all actions as interactions, and approaching these vital exchanges as opportunities to give more than to take. We affirm all of life as we affirm and tend the sacred nature of our beings and bodies. When we honor our mortal forms as evolving extensions of Spirit and Earth, every bite of precious food becomes a form of communion, and every stroke of the hairbrush or deliberate rubbing of a muscle turns into a benediction of love. We are indeed the sensory organs of Gaia, and she yearns to feel pleasure through us. It is then no longer just a "meal," a "back scratching," or a "soak" that we undertake, but homage to the body that is the house and shrine of our souls. When committed to deeply and wholly, every washing functions as absolution, every group hug as a circle cast. Any night's bath can serve as a Wiccan water-sharing...or a baptismal into the ecstasy—and duties—of the mindful spiritual path.

There exists a potential for both enchantment and sacrament every time we soulfully tend and nourish the sacred body. This is true whether one is talking about conscious cooking and eating or ceremonial bathing...whether rubbing and oiling ourselves after a hard day at work, or getting together with friends to wash each other's hair with a play of herbal shampoos. We're enchanted, teased into an altered state by this most intentional application of pleasure. These are divine moments, born of love—intensely present, focused yet relaxed—folding us into a timeless experience of oneness. We're transported by the diverse flavors of our just deserts, and by the purposeful bath with its trance-dance of touch, a bewitching of suds, and the stimulation of fairy-dust powders.

Imagine, if you will, turning out the lamp and lighting the candles next to a heated tub, opening our nostrils a little wider at the scent of grapefruit and orange, a bouquet of lavender billowing out of blooming steam. Or picture, perhaps, an antique clawfoot like ours—perched outdoors overlooking the river, fire-lit beneath an impossibly star-filled sky. On a nearby rock lies a small cobalt bowl of creamy truffles to be savored once submerged in the mind-altering suds. The aroma of almond and orange draws attention to an open container of luxurious body scrub, and a celebration of grapefruit hints at the healing salts so lovingly added to the water. We ease our entire beings into the experience...and with the slow washing of the skin, we find it is the mind that is wiped clean—temporarily unclothed of both its worries and words.

And too, our slow and grateful approach to the sweltering tub would in itself be ceremony. Noticing the soft texture of the preheated towels as we set them out: praise-giving. Quieting the mind before first deciding on a soak: contemplation. The sensual mixing of oil and essences, in the days before the bath: a stirring of a cauldron of love. Selecting the herbs or gathering and drying the flowers the long Summers before: meditation. And previously planting the seeds that grew those flowers: promise and prayer!

There is perhaps no more urgent duty than the understanding and tending of self, so that we might best understand and tend our species, the rest of creation, and this living Earth! In the course of sating and nourishing our whole selves, we become adepts in what is the ancient art of sacred indulgence. We evolve as alchemists of our own existence through the mindful practice of preparing our meals, rubbing our own stiff neck, or drawing a luxuriant bath. We truly "come into ourselves" by satisfying our authentic creature needs, and ceremonializing every intentional act...by taking responsibility for adding aroma and flavor, depth and meaning, beauty and magic to what has surely become the meaningful ritual of our lives.

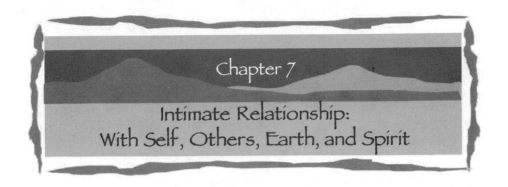

Chapter 7

Intimate Relationship: With Self, Others, Earth, and Spirit

To all our relations...

—Native American prayer

Know it or not, we relate to all that exists, and to all that has ever existed—to every thing, from the familiar and the close at hand to the eminent energies of far and distant galaxies. And thus, all things are our relatives, our extended family. Contemporary social and environmental insanity can be traced to our inability or unwillingness to recognize the myriad "others"—other people, other species, and the rocks and the rivers—as the family members they truly are, and to honor their integrity the way one would ideally honor their parents, their children, their husband, or their wife.

The return to balance requires that we recognize the fact and understand the subtleties of relationship. It requires that we relate intimately to the multiple aspects of our authentic self, to those castaway "others," to animate place and omnipresent Spirit. For the rest of Nature, intimacy is a simple matter of proximity and familiarity. For separative human kind, intimacy is also a voluntary discipline, involving our deliberate and active participation. It is a mandate, a crucial quest to really know and to love the self again, and thereby erase the destructive effects of inculcated insecurity and low self-esteem. To love the others as our self, from "homeless" panhandlers to cattails, condors, and creeks. To love the land as our source and context, and Spirit as the source and context for the living land.

Those who love their self will insist on being treated kindly and honestly, a lifestyle that's healthy, and a life with meaning. Because they are sure of their worth, they'll look for worth and value in others, and in the land. A lover might leave flowers in the path of the returning beloved, faithfully kiss his mate's eyes open each morning, or sing her praises with a mad passion. A lover of the land plants the seeds of endangered flora, embraces the sun each and every dawn without fail, composes lyrical praise for the perfumed Earth. A lover of Spirit walks in holy intercourse with this numinous quality, sensing and surrendering, learning and praising. The men and women of such passion paint in oils the telling faces and curving bodies the subjects of their affection, layer transparent pigments atop each other in a heroic effort to capture the luminosity of a cherished mountain range, to allude to the splendor of that inclusivity we call God. They dance the sacred dances and fight the essential battles to not only protect but nurture and celebrate these things that are dear to them.

Intimacy depends on a willing exchange of information and acknowledgment, opened to its full potential with the vital addition of promise and trust, and deepened by the passage of time. Such coupling benefits by both a binding agreement and a purposeful ceremony: a glad vow, an unending ritual sharing, a lasting emotional and spiritual bond. We promise to give ourselves fully to our sentient selfhood, to one another, to Earth and Spirit. We vow to respect and to nourish the beloved's unique needs and vital expression, to share adversity and fortune equally, and to defend each other's honor and form against all outside threats. In any healthy relationship, we praise the qualities and gifts of the other, consciously celebrate our relationship on a daily basis, infuse every moment with an attitude of deepest thankfulness, and seek to give back equally to the other with no resentment or restraint. Whether a relationship to persons or to the land, part of what we give back is care, and this care is most significant when it is truly heartfelt, proactive, and fully communicated.

By quieting the verbose mind and opening up to the meaning-filled signals from the rest of the living planet, we create the condition of respect necessary for complete rapport. It is our natural, if suppressed, ability to communicate with the other agents of the Earthen Whole, to serve as a conduit for their expression, and to send our own response back to that holism, informing it as it informs us. In this way, we are the instruments of the totality, and lenses benefitting from every increase in clarity. Ritual is one way of communicating to this Whole, in a deliberate exchange of sensations and responsibilities. A way of communication with the Whole through the aperture of a particular, specific place. A place we've come to know well and deeply appreciate. This is how we contact the entire universe through the eternity of a single touch. It is the way of the rest of Nature, and the way of our ancient foremothers and forefathers.

Again, all things are connected, and all exist in relationship...consciously so or not. And whether acknowledged or unrecognized, all things have significance and relevance to the other. *Conscious* relationship, however, is our *awareness* of that relevance. What we call "independence" is little more than the willful neglect of existing relationships. Environmental collapse, like the collapse of a loving relationship between two or more people, results not from some counterproductive "codependency," but rather from the pursuit of this illusory independence. All elements of the Whole depend on the rest of its constituent parts, and thus none are free of need or effect, consequence or responsibility.

Right relationship—to the inspirited Earth, to sweethearts, or to our own hungering souls—is interdependency made deliberate. It is conscious, certain relationship, holy relationship, carried forward into the wholly uncertain future. It's active, responsible, and in so many ways...touching.

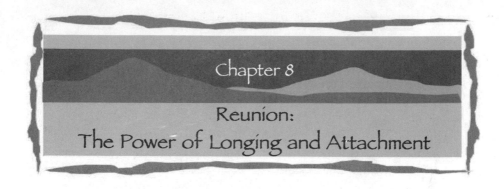

Chapter 8

Reunion:
The Power of Longing and Attachment

Spiritual awakening is frequently described as a journey to the top of a mountain. We leave our attachments and our worldliness behind and slowly make our way to the top. At the peak we have transcended all pain. The only problem with this metaphor is that we leave all the others behind. In the process of discovering our true nature, the journey goes down, not up. Instead of transcending the suffering of all creatures, we move toward the turbulence and doubt. We explore the reality and unpredictability of insecurity and pain, and we try not to push it away. At our own pace, without speed or aggression, we move down and down and down. With us move millions of others, our companions in awakening from fear. At the bottom we discover water, the healing water of compassion. Right down there in the thick of things, we discover the love that will not die.

—Pema Chodron

Longing: Yearning; wishing greatly; desiring earnestly.

Attach: To connect as an adjunct or associated part.

Union: (1) An alliance of parts; concord; harmony. (2) A state of matrimony. (3) Sexual congress; intercourse.

A prime mission of New Nature Spirituality is our learning to wholly manifest our natural, native beings. And for clarity in our path, we look to the guidance of honest, hungering wildness: all elements of the natural world driven by inherent longing, bound together through the power by attachment, empowered by the grace of love.

Eastern spiritual traditions identify longing as the cause of suffering and discontent: seeking outside of ourselves for that which we fail to find within. But longing is also a *force of connection*. It's the desire for the sensation of union, the palpable reality of wholeness, the realization of oneness. Let's acknowledge that it is longing that keeps us leaning forward, always transferring our weight to the next foot, inviting our progress. With every longing there's the possibility of us falling short, but even then the resulting pain keeps us brightly awake, real, and certain of what *matters*. Whenever we engage (not "obtain") what we long for, we're brought to the top of a hill from which we can set our sights on the next climb of desire.

It's okay to long for lovers, rivers, the healing of hurting children, the enlightenment of man, the experience of wholeness. Without longing, no bodies would come together in sweat and lather, to make it possible for conception. No soul would make the difficult passage through gestation and birth without the irrepressible longing for life. The bees would fail to make their blossom-time pilgrimages, and no sprouts would beat their soil to sun. Without our longing for clarity, we'd all be nothing but shopping-mall drones. Longing is the act of our essence reaching out a long, long ways...in order to embrace and then embody. And longing that the recipient can *depend* on is *attachment*.

We're surrounded by a dysfunctional society attached to its delusions, techno-toys, and self-destructive and environment-destroying habits. But these disempowering attachments are only a temporary human perversion of a sacred power and universal dynamic! It's because of a sense of attachment that the moon stays so near the Earth, and that the Earth maintains its orbit around the sun. Without that attachment we'd go spinning off into frozen space, with the resulting extinction of life as we know it. The atmosphere, the oceans, and countless species cling to the surface of the planet by a force that is as much attachment as gravity. Attachment is the gathering of atoms into that group hug that we've come to know as solid matter, the spin of molecules into transitional forms, and form into the transcendental immortality of art.

Mothers and fathers put up with the incessant demands of their babies, not because of any abstract sense of appropriate behavior or parental responsibility, but because they're attached. Midwestern farmers occasionally refuse to sell out to the big corporations, and Penan tribesman resist the developer's bulldozers with petitions and spears...because they're so committed to the place they call home, *attached* to a particular piece of ground.

The most credible spiritual practices and schools of psychotherapy talk about the importance of a personal centering, a gathering of our disparate parts into a formidable center, a focused presence that we call "grounding."

The word bespeaks of the connection between our authentic selves and the real and essential ground...an attachment unsevered by our leaps into the air, unbroken by our flight.

Love, like gravity, is a force of attachment. It reunites the chromosomes into the solid promise of an egg, and fuses the energies of the polar sexes into a single vibration that can cut through the thick illusion of separateness like sunbeams through the river fog at dawn. It can also drive a man to the temple of another's manhood, or coax those women together who can delight in each other's womaness. Love makes us ache when we feel separated from the beloved, whether it be our romantic partner, a precious homeland, or the experience of Spirit. And from the paunch of that ache, love draws forth the paint that fills the master canvas, the words that dance as prayers and poems, the songs that bare the soul. Love binds, not like ropes restrain a prisoner, but the way that egg binds the flour in homemade bread.

While attachment to form can lead to disappointment, attachment to essence is primary to knowing, and prerequisite to the *giving back* that is the guarantor of relationship and the requirement for oneness. Students feel attachment to their teachers, but that serves to keep their practices and their communities together. And teachers are attached...to process, without which there could be no cohesive teaching. Attached to truth. Attached to this slow unfolding of miracles! After all, attachment made deliberate is *loyalty*. Every facet and level of relating will be that much deeper, with the addition of such loyalty and the trust it engenders. This is the primary benefit of what we call polyfidelity, over noncommittal polyamory. My beautiful mate and I are open to enlarging our wildlands family to include another giving, feeling woman...not to dilute our attachment to one another, but as an expansion of ongoing loyalties and alliance, and an extension of existing promises.

Believe me, the problem is never attachment, *per se*, but what and who we choose to be attached to. We should no doubt beware of attachment to lovers that hinder our self-realization and empowerment, environments and lifestyles that fail to nourish our souls. Of careers that meet some but not all of our needs, and religions and practices that distract or detour us from answering the calling—the calling of our highest purpose.

Every mortal, inspirited human life has but a finite number of years, moments, and opportunities in which to fulfill this highest purpose. For wilder life forms, the complete fulfillment of self is guaranteed at every stage from birth to death. A flower is no more realized than a bud, a stem, or a root. But for us, life is a continual awakening and becoming that we can sabotage anywhere along the way. For human kind in particular—self-separated by the rational mind—fulfillment is a work in progress. It requires our intention, focus, persistence, creativity, and integrity. The passion that fuels long-term commitment. A core fierceness, and unstoppable love. To be truly successful in this sacred quest, we need the kind of deep humility that allows us to open up to the impressions of inspirited Nature. But we also need confidence when figuring out the difference between instincts and thoughts, the difference between what our mind might think our highest purpose is and what our heart *knows*. We are complete and fulfilled in the organic reunion we call death. The work, as I've said before, is to manifest this wholeness and rightness while alive...and while faced with the infinite challenges to our authenticity and purpose that modern civilization provides. For the sun, the quail, and the river, worth is intrinsic and absolute. For us humans, worth is an option, and fulfillment an opportunity.

Attach to what is real, even as you detach from illusion, from the culture of fear and the paradigm of greed. To experience the oneness you seek, embrace your longing as you would embrace that which you long for. And embrace the *you* that longs.

The result is reunion. And that union is love.

Chapter 9

Gaia Eros: Sacred Sexuality, Sacred Earth

It is time for us to take off our masks, to step out from behind our personas—and admit we are lovers, engaged in an erotics of place...there is nothing more legitimate and there is nothing more true.

—Terry Tempest Williams

Reclaiming a connection to our sexual beings, and to this sexualized Earth, is a very important element of both our spiritual assignment and our ecological purpose.

Sexual Nature

The New Mexico sanctuary where I write these pages has always felt "out of time," with the winds whispering of the past as they blow across these Anasazi ruins, and every day seeming like forever. There are few signs of human kind on this two-mile stretch of twisting river canyon, and yet everywhere one looks there are the signs of sentience, sensuality, and love! Primeval dramas of affection and desire unfold before our very eyes, as giant cottonwood trees rub together their pollen-laden branches. There is clearly an ancient force at work here, as seen in the ladybug beetles' swarming dogpiles, in the muskrats' nose-rubbing frivolity, and in the mating of canyon moon and purple mountain spires. We hear it in the cries of the mountain lion at the moment of orgasm, and in the gentle cooing of paired-up doves perched high atop a native mulberry tree.

It's the same everywhere in the natural world—the males of every creature species seeking recombination with the All through the union of willing flesh. Females, from flippant guppies to desirous gorillas, open like the portals of the universe in order to take into themselves the maleness that is their balance. Female bonobo apes gaily bring each other to climax without the restrictiveness of a moral primate code. Frisky coyotes rub their organs on the meadow's soft, wet grass. We sense sexuality's subtle pervasiveness in the

gently charged sexuality of youthful human bodies climbing trees or gallop-
ing on horses, and in the still hungering elder stretched out on a mountain
ledge being expertly handled by the canyon winds. We can feel it in the
fermentive warmth of the microactive soil, in the heartbeat pulse of sky-clad
mountains...and in the way an amorous river is able to touch every inch of
our skin at once! It can be found both here in this isolated wilderness, and in
community parks with rows of beckoning blossoms, or backyards abuzz with
pollen-soaked bees.

Welcome to Planet Eros, the planet of sensation and love! This is no
"dead" rock, acting as a stage for the human drama—but the terrestrial Gaia,
endlessly making love to herself through her constituent parts. This Mother
Earth is not only an ancient crone and bestower of wisdom, but also a gleeful
child, a haughty adolescent, and a lusting, fertile lover. Sexuality is her dance
of transformation, the way she changes from one stunning outfit to the next,
the fuel that powers her evolutionary drive. She is forever engaged in intercourse: the interpenetration and interrelationship of all her sacred parts. She
is bound together by intimacy, and propelled forward by love.

Pursuit and Death, Ecstasy and the World as Lover

Each one of us—every single life form and every dancing cell—is at once
both pursuer and pursued. Life seeks us out, both to make love to us and to
consume us! It is pursuit that provides the excitement, distinguishing form
from the formless, art from the artless. It affords us the equally difficult extremes of utter pain and sheer delight. We shrink from this process as if from
death itself, and it's no wonder. Whether we are caught and eaten by a large
predator, or consumed by the immensity of indomitable love, the result is the
same: the annihilation of the separative self. Indeed, those who tend to focus
most on their fear of death are usually intimidated by their sexual urges as
well, for they are the two faces of the same power. One can think of sexuality
as the animating force of evolution, the generative power that raises and
distinguishes individual elements of the Gaian body, and death as the taking
back in of that which has been extended: energy-as-form cast forward again
and again, and each time reeled back into the center. It is this necessary,
cyclical pushing and pulling that keeps the wheels of creation turning.

In denying the sexuality of the Earth, our kind finds itself in denial of
Gaia's mortal dimension. A planet impervious to the worst of what our kind
can do to it would be both sexless and lifeless. Likewise, an Earth that is
procreative and sensate is obviously vulnerable in the face of our destructive lifestyles, and thus we become personally responsible for whatever influence and effects we have. When our primal forebears restricted the
amount of trees they felled or animals they killed, or made certain activities

taboo, fear of deprivation and want weren't the only determining factors. Just as significant was their cultural perception, an attitude that this Earth is a Spirit-embodied being, sexually charged and reproductive, but also sensitive and vulnerable. In this way she is more than a "mother" Earth, but also our playmate, partner, and lover.

If we adopt this perspective—as I hold we must—it brings with it a specific code of behavior. As it would be with any lover, we're consequently busy recognizing and tending to her needs. We're called upon to adore her, to stroke her grapevine hair and assist the spread of her fertile seeds. To dedicate our poems to her, and to sing praises that bounce off the uterine caves and cornices of the nearest cliffs. And as with any lover, we're required to meticulously watch for even the most subtle indications of her suffering, and to fiercely guard against anything that could either diminish or dishonor her.

Native sexuality begins with the reinhabitation of our true sentient natures, in relationship with the natural, sensual, and inspirited world. We are, after all, not only thinking, futurist beings, but also ancient creatures of bodily delight—as integral to this inspirited, primeval planet as the granite and lava of its mountains, as rooted thousand-year-old trees and the birds that nest there. As full members, we have roles and assignments, one of which is the reuniting of human sexuality and spiritual or magical practice. In this way, it's possible for our explorations of sensation to heighten our awareness, deepen our bonds, and contribute to the healing and wholeness of the living Earth of which we are forever a part.

The Nature of Our Sexuality

Sex gets more media attention than ever, and the "civilized" remain an all-too desexualized sort. We live in a culture that glamorizes and commercializes our natural urges, while simultaneously both repressing and perverting them. The ancient pull and surge of hormonal tides have been harnessed to sell everything from aggravatingly unattractive automobiles to tacky designer shorts, while the very people who buy such things remain tragically afraid of their own innate animal sexuality, feral imaginations, and untended needs. The contemporary sexual experience is often defined more by the steamy video screen than the sweat of naked, pulsing skin. It's marked by a strangely disembodied lust—mental and competitive. Meanwhile, not enough of us are living our dreams, admitting to our needs, or openly acting on our deepest desires. While explicit Websites are more popular than ever, counselors are inundated with complaints about the lack of eroticism and romance in relationships today. And while there are images of sex on every billboard and in most magazines, we don't get to witness enough real intimacy and touch among those around us.

It is nonetheless our intrinsic, natural sexuality that can help to lead us out of the cages of our rational minds, collapsing the self-imposed walls that restrict our fullest manifestation. An intensely conscious sexual experience can reseat us in the primacy of immediate experience, and remind us of the power of our ancient, wilder selves. And those "great touchings" that include not only the lovers, but Earth and Spirit, can open us to a universe without end.

Humans have a natural infinite potential for sexual inspiration, expression, and consummation. Even within our linear modern brain there still exists a panting feral mind, one that can envision and inspire to fruition myriad combinations of bodies—male and female—of hands and mouths, feet and genitals. We are born with the capacity for boundless pleasure, and even more boundless love—restricted only by honest personal preference...and the fears and judgments of our kind.

It is our evolutionary assignment to feel not only the pain but the ecstasy of mortal life. More than anything else, human kind evolved as the sensory organs of the biosphere, Gaian "feelers," fleshy antennas communicating clear sensation to the heart of the directive Whole. Thus employed, we fulfill our mission as planetary sensitives, as the co-inhabitants of the Planet Eros, and as the conscious co-celebrants of this miracle we call life. Once we recognize that the Earth feels both pleasure and communion through us, we are more likely to make love in a sacred and magical way.

Sacred Sexuality

Sacred sexuality is the union of body and emotion, self and other, self and Earth, self and Spirit...to the benefit and glory of the Whole. This is the intent and purveyance of New Nature Spirituality, of Maypole-raising Pagans, and practitioners of Shamanism.

In sacred sexuality, the lovers embrace Spirit as well as each other. We call in the gods and goddesses, and all the elements of magic creation. In the act, our smells become one, full of charged ozone and sweetened musk. Giving pleasure, we come to share a single breath, and then a single sheath of skin as well. In the act of conscious union, we go from "they and I" to an inseparable "us," and then to the "all that is." In our bliss, ourselves expand to include and encompass all parts of continuous creation, a great bay, an arc of outstretched arms. Like the stars popping out of a blackened night, the many elements of our beings raise their faces for the kiss of life...and we are everywhere, at once.

For more than 16,000 years, human kind has been increasingly divorced from its intuitive and sensate body, increasingly oblivious to the needs of self and Earth. Practices such as Wicca and Tantra represent our kind's historic efforts to mend this dangerous schism, by reuniting sex and Spirit, sensuality and eroticism, body and soul, self and the All. And to survive, the inheritors of the future will have had to return to many of the ways of old. There will have to be no penalty for libertarianism and honest sexual expression. Dysfunctional serial monogamy will be replaced by lifelong partnerships, some exclusively between two people, some polygamous. Archaic tribal patterns will reappear, such as polyfidelity—where there is intimacy and commitment within an extended family or clan, and devotion and focus is again its own reward.

Commitments

If there is any measure of us as lovers, it is in the depth of our commitment, and the degree to which we keep our promises. It is in the conscious embrace and subsequent sharing of primal ecstasy (from the word *ekstasis*: "to be taken 'outside yourself'"). It's in our willingness to feel, and our opening to bliss. And in determination to make sure that our lover, the Earth, feels good too!

No matter what form our relationships take, their integrity, depth, and longevity depend on our ability to commit as well as nourish. We have to begin by acknowledging, embracing, and committing to Spirit, to place...and to ourselves. Only with this firm foundation can we hope to build a substantial relationship with another person. And only with the securing and celebrating of this pairing is it possible to expand the commitments to successfully include a third. I've come to realize how a monogamous relationship that is artful and prayerful can serve one's spirit better than any number of superficial or uncommitted lovers. And how being alone—and authentic, and true to the self—is preferable to a disingenuous or halfhearted affair.

The possibility exists to credibly bond with another. Or with more than one other. But the effort and emotional output increases with each addition. The onus is on us as spiritual seekers to learn how to do this honorably. Certainly there are plenty of precedents. Up until a few millennia ago, the entire history of human kind was one of group marriages, extended families, clan and tribe. The modernist culture of separation that drives us apart from each other, drives us apart from the natural world as well...and further apart from our own wilder natures.

Now it is up to us to re-create committed relationships resonant with the patterns and needs of the living Earth. The heroic calling is one of reclaiming and rejoining. We can fulfill our covenant not so much by trying out novel new forms of interaction, so much as simply remembering (re-membering: becoming members again). By remembering our place at each other's sides, here in the web of life, in the cosmos, in the continuous unfolding of our greater interwoven destinies. By remembering the importance of making promises. And by remembering to keep the promises we make.

By protecting, tending to, and loving the natural world, we will learn to be our most authentic, responsive selves. And by inhabiting our true natures, we each become like a slow burning fire—sharing many nameless temptations, thrilled with the defiant pleasures of our inherent creatureness. In time, our breath will linger on the edges of our lips like the dawn's wispy fog, as unhurried as our movements. We will access the entire universe through the Earthen womb, and the Gaian womb through this momentous, bliss-filled touch. In a healed world, we would each leave wildlife refuges and environmental art for the whole of the sweet Earth to find. We'd send her love letters made of the songs we've written and the air we've cleaned, paeans of the endangered trees we've planted, and the act of biking to a career with meaning. We'd walk with her through the gardens of our life, forgiving her everything, and giving our all. We would lie down with her, hominid bodies on tender soil, and spend long nights listening to each other breathe.

We'd greet her with a smile and a kiss every morning...and pledge her "forever" every night.

The Principles of Gaian Sexuality

- ◎ You are a component and member of the living Earth, Gaia. It is your responsibility, and your gift, to feel.

- ◎ The body is a portal to the Earth, and sacred sex a pathway into the depths of the sensate body.

- ◎ You are a sexual being, and the only shame is in failing to express and manifest your native needs, or to give to others and to Gaia the gift of your loving touch.

- ◎ Love yourself as an extension of the sacred Earth. Love others as extensions of yourself.

- ◎ Touch your body when it hurts, and give it pleasure when it doesn't. Brush your hair more slowly than usual, taking time to notice how good it really feels.

- ◎ Experiment with nontraditional sexual relations, methods, and forms. Then commit wholeheartedly to only those that best fulfill your authentic self and real needs.

- ◎ All acts are healthy that honor and gladden the beloved, and contribute to the unity of the Whole.

- Practice a combination of awareness and trust. Surrender to that which is worthy of surrendering. Allow the boundaries to dissolve, the self to pour out in reunion with the beloved.

- Quiet the mind, and perceive the beloved through each of the senses in turn. Alternately focus on them through the touch of fingertips, the scent of heated flesh, the sounds of impassioned moves and heavy breathing.

- Don't just rub the beloved's skin—pinch and cradle it, stroke and graze it.

- Make unscheduled love, out of doors and away from the clamor and distraction of your normal busy life.

- The natural world is sometimes rough, sometimes soft. Thus lovemaking should at times be hard and fast, and other times gentle and slow.

- Tune into the connection between sex and food, food and Earth.

- Indulge your dreams, for they are the dreams of this fecundate living planet.

- Make every act intimate, and every intimate act a conscious ritual of connection and delight.

- Sense an unbroken chain of lovers reaching back through the ages, paw to paw, and wing to wing.

- Experience the eroticism of a hot bath, and really get into the way a mountain creek feels as it ripples over your belly and legs. Press your body against giving, moss-covered Earth, and feel the Earth loving you back.

- Every moment is a decisive moment, and every day a series of commitments to self, other, Earth, and Spirit. Keep them!

- Tend the Goddess in every woman, the God in every man. Treat their bodies as agents and altars, their hearts as the one heart of Gaia.

*We must remember the chemical connections between our
cells and the stars, between the beginning and now. We must
remember and reactivate the primal consciousness of oneness
between all living things. We must return to that time, in our
genetic memory, in our dreams, when we were one species
born to live together on earth as her magic children.*

—Barbara Mor

It's said there are invisible threads of energy binding all the Shamans of
the world to one another...and something connects each of us as well: the
empathics and sensitives who dwell on the edge, who hear the calling, and
keep the pledge. Practitioners of authenticity and wholeness, reinhabiting
sacred self and sacred land. Seekers of significance and purpose, the last to
give up the ancient ways, and the first to explore the new. Those, it's said,
may cry too hard, or laugh too loud...that dare to care, so much! Each an
integral component, of a lineage of place holders: unbridled children and
wizened elders, willful wilders, Wiccans, and Wizards on whose souls rest
the responsibility to invoke a new/old Earth, an Earth once again green and
growing, dynamic and diverse, feral and free. Our shared ministry is this
most insistent calling. And our liturgy...is our love. Conservationists,
restorationists, and healers. Teachers, activists, and defenders. Artists, ritualists, and celebrants. All rare conduits of clarity in an age of blinding noise
and neon. We're the reinhabitants of Ectopia and Katuah, the verdant North-
east and the mountains and deserts of the mystical Southwest, of water-
sheds and wildernesses, sacred groves and organic farms. In tryst with rivers
and forests, promised to a particular valley, or courting all the Earth in a
gypsy's search for home. We're returning to an older way of being as well, to
the Great Mystery—humbled by our place in the awesome harmonic Whole.
We're determined to dance out our individual dances, never losing step with
that greater choreography of which we are a part. Like the fabled Alice, we
each pursue furtive magic through the openings in the roots of trees and the

imaginations of children. Getting down on our hands and knees, we make our way back to that Gaian Wonderland we can never really leave.

I'm excited! The energy is incredible. The transition, no matter how bright, demands that we look! Unwavering vision. Unwavering intent. I'm excited! Because I sense more acutely than ever our connection to one another, and to those spirits and life-forms we call "other." It's not really a thread that connects us after all, you know...but strands of a miraculous web. We can feel each other from great distances, through its delicate vibrations. We have only to reach out now, along these fibers, over roaring rivers, underneath a canopy of trees, in order to touch the source...through the warp and weft of interconnected consciousness. Though we may live and work in different places, we are but one tribe, with a single unified cause. Champions of sentience and sacrament, bodily extensions and voluntary agents of holy Gaian will.

The whispering river and the rustling of the leaves are this inspirited Whole, trying to get our attention. Gaia, the Earth, is speaking to us through the voices of all creation. Yes, I'm excited! I stand as if barefoot, out of breath, staring wide-eyed at the wonder of the magic exploding before us. I'm thrilled to witness this re-becoming, this song...as we're each reintegrated into the living, breathing flux, each made to feel we belong. I'm thrilled, because as loving and responsive caretakers, we're fulfilling our true evolutionary role, redeeming our species as well as ourselves.

No, we humans are not the brain of Gaia, the divine director—the anointed weaver that sets design rules for the patterns in rock, the flow of fire, the perfect twists in peach-colored seashells. But we are the voluntary magic that fills the enchanted loom, reaching out in our efforts to restore the planet. Reaching out for each other. Reaching down deep again with our splayed toes, our anxious probing roots...embracing the innermost heart of the Mother Earth, and thereby reaching out, out...until the sun encircled.

*You have to strive every minute to get rid of the life that you
have planned in order to have the life that's waiting to be
yours. Move, move, move....*

—Joseph Campbell

Since the Paleolithic time, seekers of insight, purpose, and power have
embarked on sacred quests in wild and enchanted places. Intentionally re-
moving themselves from the comfort of the familiar—from supportive family
and tribe—they set out to encounter truth and magic, to be challenged and
tested, stripped of every illusion and comfort that ever held them back. They
sought alliance with Earth and Spirit, and the personal power or medicine
needed to do what is right. And they went in hopes of a gift: an omen or sign,
an essential lesson, a spirit ally or animal guardian, a revealing of dormant
magic skills...and always, a deeper vision of their self, their role, and their
purpose.

This deliberate engagement with being and meaning was common to the
primal ancestors of every race on nearly every continent: The intense initiation rights of the Lacandon Mayan warriors of Guatemala and the Yoruba
priestesses of beautiful Africa. The Hopi child at the onset of puberty, facing
weeks in the dark recesses of a ceremonial underground kiva. The blue-eyed
Sami Shamans of mountainous Scandinavia, laying in an icy pit until finally
earning the curiosity and assistance of the gods. The Aborigine of Australia's
outback, embarking on long spirit-filled journeys they call "walkabout." The
Cheyenne seeker, sitting cross-legged for days and nights on end atop the
highest wind-blown peak. Such quests might be rites of passage marking a
girl's transition into womanhood at the first sign of menses, or her *eventual*
shifting into the wizened ranks of cronehood at the end of her moon cycle.
Or they may be undertaken during times of personal quandary, to reconnect
with the dear departed, solve a problem, meet a need. It is a furthering of
commitment to the lifelong quest that is life—ever seeing more, understanding more, feeling more, caring more.

With New Nature Spirituality we don't duplicate any indigenous ritual, tradition, or way of questing. As eclectics, we might study the many historical examples, but as intuitives we depend on sensing the direct revelatory will of Spirit and Nature for direction as to the form and content of our sacred efforts. For example, nothing about the way we do Spirit Quests at our Earthen Spirituality Project sanctuary is Native American per se, which also respects Native Americans' concerns over "cultural appropriation." Instead, we are instructed by the same holy and whole Source that once informed and inspired the original inhabitants of this most enchanted canyon, and likewise, all magical peoples in all places and times.

Many of us never think about doing anything like a retreat or quest until we've barely survived a disease that could have killed us, or until we've had a series of failed romances or aborted careers that leave us confused and wanting. Certainly those who are most susceptible, and most ready, are often the few who are at the point of breakdown and rebirth. But there is no one alive who couldn't benefit from a soul-affirming quest for truth and being, at any time. And the survival of our kind—as well as the survival of so many other species and the ecosystems that support them—may depend on each and every one of us making repeated forays into the unfamiliar regions of self and place. Only when we've regained the sense of self-love and Gaian assignment common to the rest of Earthen life can we hope to have the clarity to repair our lives and heal our world.

The Spirit Quest Defined

As taught and practiced here at the sanctuary, a Spirit Quest involves a minimum seven-day commitment. This includes: time for presence, sharing, and orientation; a day gathering wood and tending fire for a hot medicine sweat; up to four days and nights of fasting outside on your own; and a day or two for slow assimilation and integration of the various experiences and lessons.

The Site

The most successful quests are undertaken in the wilderness, open to the instruction of the natural world, and free of the distractions and contrivances of civilization. Anywhere in the natural "undeveloped" world one can both tap the wisdom of the Earth, and heal from the effects of our obsessions, denial, habits, and fears. And all the more so in those notable spots where power and clarity are most accessible and even inescapable.

Anywhere we go, we are likely standing on ground that was once conse-crated by the aboriginal peoples who preceded us, and through this awareness we can align ourselves with the sensibilities of those seekers who came before. Stepping where the Goths once stepped, dancing where the Aztecs danced, we are pressed to the same level of sensitivity and awe, to the same depths of humility and respect. And the forms of the landscape and the vagaries of water-sheds that brought the ancients to these places, continue to act like a magnet for the attuned seeker of today. High storm-swept peaks, unusual rock forma-tions, and the confluence of rivers are typically places of power and visitation. As are any womb-like caves, the furthest projections of land into the pound-ing ocean swells, and the places where artesian springs bubble forth from their crest of fertile ground.

The canyon where we host our Spirit Quests is filled with the abandoned house sites of the Sweet Medicine People, also called the "Mogollon," and the sanctuary itself is home to the largest ceremonial kiva site in the region—further indication of its spiritual significance to those who preceded us. And to this day, a place of seldom equaled beauty and inescapable truths. For our canyon questers, there are a number of stunning pink and purple cliffs to choose from, pock marked with rain-sculpted depressions, and featuring rocks that look like animals or like faces looking back at us. For shade there are alligator bark junipers and majestic pines, some draped with wild grape ar-bors glinting emerald in the first morning light. In a way, making it here to the canyon is a quest in itself. Because of its distance in miles from any city or airport and the busy schedules that everyone keeps, it requires unusual de-termination to make the long trip from wherever. In addition, a potential quester can usually feel the power of the revelations that await them, and sense the implications and responsibilities they bring. Coming to the canyon for medicine work is an act of uncommon vision, courage, and follow-through.

The Fast

Fasting is an extremely valuable aspect of the meaningful quest. A fast is an opportunity to cleanse the lens of perception, at the same time as the body. It exposes and challenges our attachment to comfort, while heighten-ing all our senses including the so-called "extrasensory." And as with other aspects of the quest, it serves to remind us that we are infinitely stronger than we think.

The Medicine Sweat

Before embarking on a wilderness quest, it's essential to first undergo a cleansing sweat in a heated lodge.

As with other practices humans have devised to help them stay aligned with the Earth and Spirit that sustain them, the medicine sweat is common to the majority of our ancestors. Whether it is a hole dug into the ground, embryonic bent willow lodges covered with hides, or the raised rock saunas of the pantheist Vikings, our kind has almost universally sought out the scalding testament of heated rocks splashed again and again with ladles of crystal mountain water. The effect of the sweat is not only to cleanse the skin, but to cleanse the mind of useless thought, purifying the human soul in preparation for its purposeful interaction with holy Spirit.

In the canyon, we spend an entire day collecting firewood, and asking various rocks if they'd be willing to serve the intentions of the sweat. The fire pit is dug out, and the walls of the low-roofed lodge covered. By midnight the fire is lit, and it's tended until the sky begins to lighten. Red pulsing rocks are rolled out of the fire with a stick, and are moved with a pair of old deer antlers the rest of the way to the waiting hole in the center of the lodge. Somewhere around four large or eight medium sized rocks are used in each of four different rounds.

With the questers inside and the door flap sealed tight, a sprinkling of sage and copal sends sweet smudge into the air, followed by the first splash of water on the wildly sizzling rocks. Adding a little more water at a time, the heat is brought up to the point where we don't think we can stand anymore, and then we add still a little more. Between each of the rounds we exit, skin still steaming, and plunge into a hole in the chilly river of mirrors.

The last round is timed so that it ends just as the morning sun first touches the cliffs above. Crawling out of the dampness and heat is like the passage from the uterus into a world made new again. Every sight and color seems freshened; every smell brightened. The once cluttered mind shines as transparent as an opened window, and as glad as a child. The sensate body is ascendant, and the giving heart reigns.

Effect and Commitment

It's easy for one to imagine that they've failed their quest, having been trained to doubt ourselves and question our worth from an early age. But in the Spirit Quest there is no such thing as "failure." Even if we come down early, we are marked by a depth of experience that we can use in measuring every other aspect of our lives. If we find we're unable to escape the monarchy of the mind, we will at least have identified it as the frightened and counterproductive despot it can be.

It's easy for someone used to the special effects of videos or the easy hallucinations of drugs to be disappointed if no eagle lands on their knee and tells them what they want to hear, or if the sky fails to split apart at the approach of a procession of angels. We may be unimpressed at first with the seeming commonplace nature of unfolding experience. Compared to the rapid-fire images of modern entertainment, the real world may seem to move in excruciatingly slow motion. But then, at last it moves slow enough so that the very idea of time is suspended, and we get a taste of eternity—the eternal vibrant now!

On the other hand, while on quest, no event or feeling is insignificant: bugs inscribing circles in the dust as they do their mating dance. The play of feathered clouds. The intercourse of sight and sound. Every impression, every seeming coincidence, every emotion that arises, tells a part of the story of the realized self—in a vital relationship to all that is.

Oddly enough, it's by going on a quest by ourselves that we learn we're never really alone. The quest links us to a lineage of questers and seekers, and to every other constituent of this living, dancing matrix. To the distant past and hopeful future, and to the irreplaceable present tense. The quester is gifted with heightened awareness, and with it comes the responsibility to act. For every gift: a commitment!

The Quest strips away illusion and denial, reuniting us with our authentic selves: our feelings, instincts, needs, gifts, abilities, hopes, and dreams. It leads us out of the cage of the fearful, rational mind and back into the intuitive matrix of Earth and body, heart, and soul. Inevitably, those parts of ourselves that we've either lost or suppressed resurface in the light of the vital Quest experience. We welcome back the more sensitive, wonder-filled sides of our essential beings...and discover the kind of strength that comes with our inherent vulnerability. We come to feel blessed by our struggles as well as our gifts, awash in gratitude, anointed in love, and devoted to that which matters most.

We are emptied, enrolled, and fulfilled...in this ancient quest for true being and most meaningful purpose. And connected...to all there is, to all that we can be.

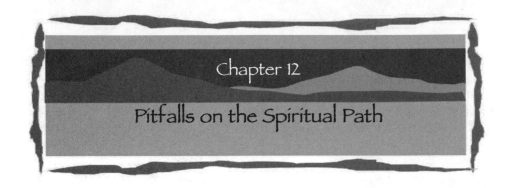

*If you want the kernel you must break the shell. And therefore
if you want to discover nature's nakedness you must destroy
mere symbols, and the farther you get in the nearer you come
to its essence. When you come to the One that gathers all
things up into itself, there you must stay.*

—Meister Eckhart

Otherwise benign new spiritual and magical practices can suffer from some of the same pitfalls as conventional organized religions. Fortunately, once we're aware of these diversions, we can make the informed choices that reunite us with Gaia, the inspirited world, rather than those that contribute to our estrangement.

In my life of pilgrimage, the voices of Earth and Spirit have repeatedly contradicted what I've read, was taught, once thought, and so badly wanted to believe. Thus, as I became a teacher myself, I deferred again and again, not to presumed authorities or established traditions, but to the actual Source of every real truth they contain. Our realization of wholeness/holiness begins not in contemplation or conclusion, but in a great listening. It begins in a vulnerable condition of openness, with fierce focus, gentle humility, and the overwhelming gratitude that makes us worthy of such gifts.

The Myth of Light Versus Dark

An all-white piece of paper is blank. It's the relationship of dark and light that defines form and makes movement visible to the human eye. Our lives are defined not only by moonless nights and sun-drenched days, but also by what artists call "chiaroscuro": the delicate interplay of dark and light brought about by subtly shifting shadows.

To make sense of what is illuminated, one must explore the dark depths of its meaning and its being. There's really nothing intrinsically good or evil about either. Even as the usual metaphor, the darkness serves us in the form of insightful pain, comforting silence, the stillness between periods of tiring activity, the death that begets life...and the blackness that gives birth to light.

The Problem With "Higher" and "Lower"

We have to be careful about adopting a hierarchical model for consciousness and our progress on the spiritual path. Using a scale of "higher" and "lower" is in the tradition of kings and peons, popes and vassals—a tradition of judging, exalting, and condemning.

We speak of "high-minded" ideals, "higher civilizations" and "lowly primitives," "higher" chakras and those base "lower" ones. Modern science, organized religion, and the New Age largely share the attitude that humans are a "higher" life form...rather than us being uniquely assigned but fully interconnected and cosmically, spiritually, and energetically equal to all the other vital forms of the Gaian/universal Whole. We're taught that mammals are "higher" (and thus more worthy of protection) than reptiles, that reptiles are higher than insects, and that the lowest of low—microbes—have no right to life at all.

In reality, the Earth is spinning in space, with no fixed "up" or "down." All people regardless of their race or their "level" of sophistication, all life forms, and even rock and soil and river are interwoven on the shared plane of Gaian matter, and in the shared depths of spiritual/evolutionary purpose.

In order for something to be "greater," it must first be separate. And in matters of Earth and Spirit, there is no such thing as separation.

Waiting for Salvation

While alternative spirituality has largely turned away from the big religions' reliance on a separate and external God coming to make things all right, there's still a tendency to look outside ourselves for something to blame, and something to save us. We can't help but desire being let "off the hook," relieved of responsibility for our condition, our acts, our failed or fulfilled dreams. New soteriological dogma tries to shift this responsibility from the individual seeker to malevolent spirits, guardian angels, or manipulative "extraterrestrials."

In truth, there's no getting around the work. The assignment is ours. No one else is to blame, and we accept our share of the credit.

Imagining That We're the Directors

There's a flip side to expecting someone or something to absolve us of guilt or bail us out of our predicaments. While the dominant religious paradigm talks about God-given "dominion" over the Earth and all it's plants and creatures, the language of New Nature Spirituality refers to benign "shepherding." But either way, we're being told that we have the wisdom to make decisions about the life and death of other species, and to determine the direction of evolution. There are naturalists who accept that the Earth as a self-regulating system (the so-called "Gaia Hypothesis"), but insist that we were designed to be the "brains" of the living planet. They see humanity as the directors of life and process, and collectively, as the organ of judgment and decree.

If they could, the mountains, the endangered redwoods, and the vanishing wolves would tell us that we are neither. The canyon, the river, and the elk would rather we embrace our true evolutionary role as Gaian sensors, providing information to the planetary "all" by feeling, emoting, and responding to the conditions of the changing environment. Our shared purpose is caring. Our purpose is *love*.

The "Spaceship" Earth

The major religions describe the Earth as an incidental stage for the acting out of the human play, the inconsequential testing lab and proving grounds of our benighted kind. Equally insulting is the notion of the Earth as a "spaceship." Spaceships are lifeless and soulless containers, whereas the Earth is a living composite—less a vessel than a seed, sailing not only through space, but through time.

The Cult of Mind

The idea of an external and judgmental God has been slowly usurped over the last hundred years; unfortunately, not by a God that is both female and male, that includes rather excludes creation. Instead, what we've witnessed is the ascension and glorification of the rational human mind. And it's not only the atheists, scientists, pragmatists, and materialists who have joined the cult. All too often the mind is treated as the center of our being, when it's primarily just a word processor. The mind is naturally employed and best redeemed as a translator and spokesperson for the house of our empathy and love, as a servant of the still feeling human heart.

Preoccupation With Past and Future

While alternative spiritual thought often extols a mindful Buddhist "here and now," there's a countercurrent of distraction from the vital present, a preoccupation with "future states" and "past lives."

Our spiritual essence and energy is recycled back into the sacred soup, into the holy whole-ly All; and as such, we have access to memories from all of creation and not just a lineage of dramatic reincarnations. But even with this great connection to a four and a half billion–year history of creation, our duty is the immediate mindful moment. Nothing that happened in the past is an excuse for current predicaments, nor are solutions in the hands of the future.

And whatever we accomplish later in our lives, whatever plateaus of revelation and experience we eventually reach, whatever ways later generations might manifest and excel...will depend on our sentient inhabitation of *now*.

Omens, Fate, and Destiny

There's no doubt that other life forms and the rest of the living world are endlessly communicating to us, imparting value and experience, setting examples and offering inspiration. There is indeed significance to everything that happens, and a lesson in every experience. The pitfall is that omens are so easily misinterpreted by a mind that seeks predetermined answers. And at best, omens are no more than signposts at various forks on the spiritual path. It's still our choice and our responsibility, because every moment is a decisive moment.

It's too easy to credit fate for our successes and failures. What we're really dealing with is destiny. Fate as a concept is absolute, and thus an easy cop-out; whereas destiny requires our conscious and active participation. Destiny is our personal Gaian song, but it remains our choice whether we get up and dance to it. It's a collaborative effort, between the wave, the opportunity, the momentum...and the human volunteer. It's embracing all that you are, and all that you can be, in alignment with the intentions and forces of Earth and Spirit.

The Cult of Happiness

In the pursuit of happiness, some alternative spiritual practices recommend we avoid negative influences. However, it's exposure to the so-called "negative" that tests and fortifies the positive. Systems, habits, and regulations are potentially more dangerous to one's spiritual path than chaos or disruption could ever be. Besides, the Earth teaches that happiness is too easy a goal for our fleeting finite lives, too low a mark for our aims, too little to ask for one's primary prayer. Better we covet childish exhilaration and sensual ecstasy, strive for quiet contentment and raucous excitement, pray for the realization of our truest, responsive, sensate selves! Better we seek the fullest expression of that being, suffer the price of our increased awareness, and bear the utter joy that is then our reward! After all, joy and suffering are polar twins, pointing to the same capacity and willingness to feel. Together they widen the scale, expand the measure of how alive we truly are! Happiness is the mind freed of immediate worries, the basket of our lives emptied of all disruptive input. Joy, on the other hand, is an ecstatic disruption—that together with longing and sorrow, fills that basket to the brim.

Happiness is comparatively shallow and inevitably conditional; whereas joy is so deep it remains undefeated, even with our honest embrace of the saddest of events. Gaia teaches us to embrace both, and to give thanks. For to really enjoy, one must fully *enjoin*...and fully *rejoice*!

Equating Difficulty With Misdirection

One way in which the old and new spiritual paradigms differ is that the former assumes the more difficult something is, the better indication we're doing what we're "supposed to," while the latter holds that if something is inordinately hard, it "wasn't meant to be."

While the magical and spiritual paths provide us with both, neither difficulty nor ease are clear indications that we are doing either right or wrong. Even while acting impeccably, we'll find ourselves equipped with advantages as well as disadvantages, blessed with both struggle and opportunity.

The Vilification of Death and Illness

Of course our energy, postures, lifestyles, attitudes, and intentions affect our state of health. But many old and new teachings take this to the extreme, implying that all illness is preventable by purifying spiritually. The result is that one can end up equating illness with the level of spiritual advancement, with the sickest made to feel to blame for their maladies, and death seen as a defeat rather than as a teacher and unifier. In New Nature Spirituality we know that while healing one's ills is important, so is learning from every disability or illness.

A Goal of No Suffering

Religion has long promised an end to suffering in the "life after death," while some new dogma promises techniques to rid us of suffering right now. Unfortunately, "no pain, no gain" is true in matters of emotion and Spirit as well as bodybuilding. Pain is not punishment, but a call to *attend*. Likewise, suffering is not our duty or karma, but rather the balance to exquisite pleasure. It is the counterweight against which we pull, and it is that pulling that provides the strength of our joy. Suffering is not how we pay the fine for past crimes, but how we pay the dues of our membership in the roles of the aware. It is the price of sensation, and part of the reward of being alive.

Transmutation of Desire and the Distrust of Instinct

Most forms of alternative spirituality, like conventional religiosity, teach that desire is an unruly child that doesn't know what's best for it, that the analytical left brain should have veto power over intuition, and that our instincts are "animal" impulses we must struggle to overcome.

Priests, politicians, and gurus alike distrust the power of our inherent, native intuition. And perhaps they should, because it is what warns us when we're being disempowered, and what begs us to strike out against what binds us. It's a red light designed to warn us...about the hours of our lives burned up without engaging in truly meaningful activity, the days spent stuck in artificially lit boxes, our Earth-damaging or soul-deadening careers, and any partners we might live with who don't love and honor us like they should. Intuition is simply "body smarts," ancient corporeal knowledge directing us to what best serves our real needs and authentic selves, and away from anything failing to serve us in this way. It's fulfilled by mindful food gathering whether in a store or a field, but it recoils at standing in line. It's attracted to learning, but is suspicious of schools.

Our deepest instincts are the still-valid messages echoing the cumulative experience of our evolutionary past, and the forward-looking intentions of the Whole. While ideas can be independent of and even contrary to the direction of Earth and Spirit, instincts are inseparable aspects of manifest Gaian will.

Teachers can pass on all the best processes in the world, but we still need to develop intuition and instinct in order to personally know how, where, and when to apply them.

Ritual as Retreat

Both spontaneity and repetition can be valuable tools of the spiritual path. One is about responding heartfully in the moment, the other is about the deliberate deepening of intention and prayer.

Repetition is good for ritualizing our intentional acts, and is particularly important for the undisciplined and indulgent modern person. But ever-relevant Nature teaches that when ritual becomes unconscious and rote, it loses its meaning. And that when it loses meaning, when it becomes more theatre than palpable magic, it isn't ritual anymore—it's *habit*. In addition, patterns, schedules, and constraints can become yet another escape from individual responsibility and unsettling but necessary change. Thus, for the most scheduled and organized of seekers, disruption can be medicine, and the collapse of one's patterns and plans, a cure.

The Myth of "Complete" Teachings

There are no closed systems in the universe, other than the entirety of the universe itself. All the rest are subsets, acting in reciprocal relationship. Thought patterns, beliefs, practices, human beings, entire bioregions, even the Earth are all open systems that shed substance, energy, and ideas, while constantly taking on new material. We're only complete as part of this greater Whole, in connection to all that enjoins and contains us, in intimate consort with all that is.

Likewise, no matter what our teachers or religious leaders might tell us, the borders of all teachings are mutable and transgressable. They're subject to new input, evidence, and revelation. It's in this way that illusions are shattered, while authentic truths are not only reaffirmed but expanded and augmented.

All real truths are inviolable and insoluble pieces of an ever-evolving, ever-manifesting puzzle. Because truths are multidimensional, a serious seeker is forever turning them over, exposing previously unrecognized aspects and applications. There's an element of creative disruption, and a correct decision becomes more difficult whenever we see the myriad sides of a situation, the myriad overlapping interactive truths...*but there are no contradictions in truth itself.* On the farthest side of each piece, one finds not its opposite, but those equally valid qualities that provide for balance.

Complete understanding is impossible for us, but a sense of completeness and connection are not. The more sides we unveil, the better we can see how each truth fits into the bigger picture, and understand its place and ours in this magical universe, in/of the living Earth, with/in those reoccurring patterns some call destiny or fate.

When a plant stops growing, it dies. So it is with religions, philosophies, sects, and denominations. The beauty of a healthy teaching is that it's admittedly, forever, incomplete—ever-expanding like the universe, a learning practice as humble and resolute as a wizened sorcerer, as wide-eyed and open-hearted as a newborn child.

The Pursuit of Detachment

Both the conventional and new spiritual paradigms preach detachment from the material body, and the material Earth, while the Earth teaches and embodies attachment, intercourse, and interdependence. Healthy longing is attraction to what is most real, meaningful, and needed...resulting not in aching discontent but in reconnection and wholeness.

The Misinterpretation of Peace

According to conventional organized religions, inner peace results from fully adopting and obeying their dogma, and surrendering to their avatar. In some forms of alternative spirituality, inner peace is considered synonymous with tranquility. But in Gaian terms, peace is the state of being sated and centered—even when faced with deprivation and turmoil. Peace is a deep contentment that arises from self-knowledge and self-acceptance. It's an inner balance that, like a ship's gyroscope, ensures personal peace no matter how we're tossed about by the storms that rage around us.

Peace is more a product of spiritual focus and commitment than it is of agreement. We are most at peace with ourselves and our beliefs when they can stand the challenge of detractors, defy consensus, survive disagreement, and continue to grow without outside affirmation or support.

Inner peace results not from accomplishment so much as from the knowledge that we have done our best...and that we have done so for all the most generous and significant of reasons. It comes from giving more than others may be able to receive, and being comfortable with accepting what others have to give. From a feeling of connection to the rest of the living world. And from fulfilling our most meaningful purpose.

The Goal of Transcendence

In the old paradigms, transcendence comes with our death and resurrection. For the new, it comes through practice, in this life. For Gaia, there is nothing to transcend, and nowhere to go.

We need to exceed our imaginary limits at every opportunity, sense the ways in which our energy and soul extend beyond the boundaries of the skin and into every being making up this Gaian Whole, the being that reaches beyond the constraints of time to a condition of eternal oneness. But the concept of transcendence is a dangerous one. At its extreme, it encourages detachment from the sacred, sensual, mortal body, and estrangement from our primordial desires. The Earth is desperate for us to learn how to reinhabit our bodies and our land, not how to transcend them.

To transcend is to leave, while we've yet forgotten how to *be*, and forgotten how to *stay*. In reality, the most important place for us to go is right here, experiencing our vital presence and total connection to the unfolding universe, taking responsibility for our lives and our planet.

The most mystical of all travel is that return trip, to precious sense of place, and authentic sensual self. As always, the truly spiritual path is the one that leads us back to the instructions of Earth and Spirit—the path leading home.

Chapter 13

Under the Juniper Tree: An Interview on
Buddhism and New Nature Spirituality

*I think the real miracle is not to walk either on water or in thin
air, but to walk on earth.*

—Thich Nhat Hahn

Author interviewed by Maya, an intern at the Earthen Spirituality Project,
on December 14, 2000.

Maya: Your writings and teachings celebrate Nature as the preeminent
source of instruction and inspiration. Much of your work has a
decidedly Buddhist ring to it.

**Jesse Wolf
Hardin:** Every insight that "rings true"—no matter what form it might
take—arises from the same source: all-inclusive Spirit, most intimately embodied in and expressed through the manifestations of
the natural world. Nature is perhaps the clearest channel to the
wisdom and experience of Spirit, where truth is revealed in its
current, native context. And my decades of living close to the
Earth have shown me the ways in which every creature is a per-
fected being, every fox a seer, every bear a bodhisattva, every
hummingbird a messenger of enlightenment and rebirth. Challenging revelations—and certain humility—"under the juniper
tree."

Among the world's major religions, Zen Buddhism and the
Tao Te Ching come closest to explaining the world as it's been
revealed to me by Spirit...through this living planet, through a
particular river canyon and the specific sacred site I'm given to
resacrament and restore. Buddhism and Paganism/New Nature
Spirituality share a primary focus on relationship...and at their
best, on the importance of "right action."

M: Tell me what first attracted you to Buddhism.

JWH: It began with a pilgrimage to see Alan Watts as a "troubled" teen, pursuing my visions and hopes on an unregistered motorcycle. I was influenced by those who spoke of biodiversity as well as Dharma, recognizing the ways in which both the quality of wildness and the fact of wilderness are essential to the authenticity, vitality, and sanctity of the Great Wheel of Life. And I began to understand the resonance I felt with Buddhist sensibilities, largely thanks to the works of Gary Snyder, Bill Devall, and Joanna Macy.

M: What do you consider your life's purpose?

JWH: Furthering truth and awareness. Demonstrating gratitude for every gift, lesson, and challenge. Employing magic in service.

M: What kind of service?

JWH: To the greater self, the Whole of imperiled creation. Service motivated by compassion, expressed through art, and manifest in deeds.

My intent is the same whether I am writing and teaching, or replanting indigenous trees: to mend my connection to the informative, inspirited world...and to assist others as they progress from self-made strangers to committed familiars. My words are trail markers on the wilderness path, the spiritual path leading us from imagined separation into fully conscious, participatory wholeness.

M: So much suffering is a result of that separation, and even more so, a result of the hatred separation creates.

JWH: I don't see suffering as a product of hatred so much as a gift of love. We suffer physical pain, because we are blessed with and have learned to love sensation. Our loneliness is love—seeking affirmation. To empathize with the suffering of others is an act of love and compassion. When we are fully conscious, fully mindful, we come to ache for the indigenous plants and animals displaced by our cities, suffer for the extincted species and depleted forests—out of a great and personal love. And at the same time, just as the resistance and challenge of a load makes one stronger and more deliberate, the suffering we bear contributes to love's force and assignment. For the Buddha, suffering was an aide and teacher, the inspiration for his divine compassion.

As you know, social, environmental, psychological, and spiritual imbalance result not from some "original sin," but "original separativeness": the tragic moment of our first perceptual, emotional, and spiritual distancing. Separativeness is the capacity and tendency to feel separate, and to act independently, from the rest of the holy Gaian Whole.

M: If there is any "law of Nature," it would be the law of oneness, where all things seek their true nature and ultimate unity. One of our traditions uses a metaphor for interconnection, in which every aspect of the Whole reflects all the others....

JWH: Yes, Indra's net—deftly woven by purposeful Spirit, working through the arms of an enchanted spider. Its countless junctures are bejeweled with the morning's dew. Nature has no "laws," only intention, direction, and pattern. Gaian Dharma is the mandate of interrelationship, interest, interpenetration, intercourse, and interdependence...of reciprocity and responsibility.

M: How do you define *responsible* and *reciprocal*?

JWH: The principle of reciprocity requires we give back to the Whole an equal amount to the gift of increased awareness. Consciousness and compassion make us participants, whether we like it or not. And they come with certain attendant responsibilities: the ability and willingness to respond. To respond to the plight of abused wives, starving children, and warehoused convicts. Or of extirpated wolves, mountains ravaged by strip mines, rivers stopped up with dams that no salmon can climb.

Faced with the ongoing despoiling of the entire sacred planet, we are moved to act far more decisively than if it were only our lives or belongings at stake. The practitioners of "engaged Buddhism" are proactive in seeking ways to create the conditions for a healthy Earth, as well as a peaceful inner center. Recognizing the impermanence of form can cause us to treasure all forms, rather than becoming indifferent to the fate of any. To go with the flow is to surrender to the intention, direction, pace, and patterns of Earth-embodied Spirit—not to give up to the forces of distraction and destruction.

M: In some ways, though, doesn't activism increase resistance and conflict, and therefore separation?

JWH: Should a commitment to ahimsa preclude resistance—when the failure to intercede might cause the greatest harm of all?

     Instead of acting to ease the suffering of an "other," the social activist can treat a disease of the whole. Instead of acting for the good of some externality, the environmental activist can act to protect the integrity of one's greater, Gaian self.

M: In your book *Kindred Spirits: Sacred Earth Wisdom*, you discuss plants and animals as teachers, skills for reconnection and Earth stewardship, and what you call personal and global "rewilding."

JWH: Western civilization has maldefined "wild," equating it with things that are explosive, out of control, dangerous....In reality, wildness is the quality of authentic being and true Nature exemplified by the dance of wilderness. And wildness is our natural, mindful, and responsive state as well. It is an active and hyperconscious state of oneness with body, soul, and place. It is the embodiment of our desires, needs, sensations, intuition, instincts, and dreams. To be wild is to be intolerant of those things that threaten life, that rob us of responsibility, or dishonor the sacred, and to insist on a great healing, nourishing, bonding, and celebration.

M: I love the whole idea of a conscious, compassionate, beneficent rewilding. But at the same time, isn't tolerance an important quality to develop, and essential to any relationship?

JWH: What is essential to healthy relationships is recognition of the self in others, respect for that which is unrecognizable...and right response. To tolerate is to accept or ignore dissonance, harm, or dishonor.

     One ignores, denies, or represses—rather than "tolerates"—aspects of the self they're uncomfortable with. One can only be tolerant of that which they imagine to exist outside their self. In this way, toleration can actually reinforce perceptual duality.

M: Jack Kornfield writes that "without tolerance we would have a society of perpetual conflict, a world of sectarianism and tribalism, of warfare and genocide."

JWH: A world of tolerance may be one where humans have learned to set aside their native preferences and rhythms in order to function in an increasingly abstract and joyless lifestyle—in a landscape largely covered in concrete and asphalt, where our plant teachers, animal role models, and sacred places of power have been replaced by an artless commercial culture and an endlessly expanding human population.

To accept something is to acknowledge the reality of it, and good or bad, to take it into ourselves, to own our connection to even the most destructive and reprehensible. We accept every being, circumstance, disturbance, and difficulty as a gift.

Most of the differences we're talking about here are a matter of vocabulary. I'm sure Kornfield would agree that accepting the reality and lessons of something doesn't mean we do any less than all we can to disarm that which is dangerous, heal that which is unwhole...that we bring silence to cacophony, and truth to silence.

As for tribalism—while it helps make sectarian conflict possible, it is also a refuge of cultural diversity, Earth ethics, and personal codes of integrity and honor. Tribalism is as much a part of any global return to balance and oneness as it is a source of difference and contention.

It seems to me that the absence of conflict is not the same as peace. Peace is contentment and conscious oneness in the face of natural and sometimes inevitable conflicts. In addition, conflict—like accord—can serve strength, understanding, and growth.

M: What do you mean by "vocabulary"? Are you talking word definition, or relative context?

JWH: Both. Even when we share a common language, history, place, and circumstance, the insights revealed by Spirit through the portal of the Earth are expressed in the vernacular of our subjective vantage, in the vocabulary of our personal experience. All the truths of the universe are available to us all the time, in a depth and quantity equal to our capacity to hear, house, and accommodate them. We set them to the words, rhythms, and tones available to us, express them in the colors of our individual presence and principles.

M: American Buddhism is different from that of Asia, and the woman meditating next to me has a practice that is in some ways unique to her alone.

JWH: I can sympathize with spiritual leaders who deride the indulgence, "pop sensibility" and neglect of tradition that occurs when a practice is adapted for new places and new times. But at the same time, the ability of a practice to reconnect us to self, Earth, and Spirit is dependent on its subjective relevance. In New Nature Spirituality we open up to the original source of all insight and connection, to the instructions of Spirit and place. We join the ancient Native American elders and Druidic priests, the Hourani Shamans of Ecuador and the holy Lamas of Tibet in calling forth a connection and re-creating a practice that is true to our mixed heritage and found homes, true to the current needs of self and Earth in these contemporary times.

Chapter 14

Mulberry Truths

Convince me that you have a seed there, and I am prepared to expect wonders.

—Henry David Thoreau

There's no greater repository of instruction and inspiration than the natural world. Search and you will find courage and compassion in the acts of animals, contentment in the embrace of shifting clouds or a turquoise sea...and enlightenment in the lessons of a single mulberry tree.

Well-managed orchards are impressive, but the rareness of wild mulberry trees make them the most special of all:

> Seek friends and lovers, causes and careers, places and moments that embody character and meaning—not those that conform best or produce the most.

Hikers that were busy talking have been known to walk right under a tree's branches without noticing its berries:

> The entire natural world is constantly trying to engage, instruct, and nourish us. There are lessons, gifts, and miracles all around, if only we'd wake up and open to them.

Turn or duck your head even the slightest bit, and you may spot berries you hadn't previously seen:

> In life, the slightest change in perspective often bears fruit.

The sweetest berries nest high in the tree, and it can be risky getting to them:

> Special rewards come to those who are willing to risk a fall.

At the same time, we often overextend ourselves in order to pick what looks like a special berry, only to find sweeter ones right under our nose:

> The distant and exotic look good from a afar, but often the greatest treasures in life are close at hand.

We'd likely hurt ourself if we tried to get out to the berries nested on the end of some slender branch. But then again, we may be able to pull the branch closer instead:

> It can look as though the things we want in life are out of our reach. But sometimes by staying true to our values, beliefs, assignments, and purpose, we can pull closer those people and situations we desire.

When high in the tree, the careful gatherer keeps a firm hold with whichever hand isn't busy picking:

> When taking risks and making changes—when projecting into the future or reaching an arm out into the unknown—it's wise to hold on with the other...maintaining a grip on the here and now, the real and reliable, the tested and true.

Test the branch that you take before putting all your weight into it:

> If we don't want to fall hard, we should carefully consider any forks in the trail of life before fully committing ourselves.

If the tree gets no rain it will die—but if overwatered, its fruits turn out colorless and bland:

> A person, whether a child or an adult, needs sustenance and attention. But those who are fussed over and smothered, who never learn to do without, are often the least interesting and effective people.

From a single branch, broken by the snow, two new branches grow:

> If our lives are rooted in truth and place, trauma brings about new awareness and growth. We branch out in response to each broken effort, doubling the number of approaches and attempts.

Some wild foods spoil more quickly than others. This is why ground squirrels carry most of the acorns they gather home to their nest, but eat all berries they can find:

> In life, there are times to store and save, and times to gorge.

For every season of giving, there are months of preparation:

> The mulberry only produces berries for a brief three-week period, while the rest of the year it rests, draws sustenance from the Earth, mends its wounds, and replenishes its vital sugars.

Sometimes the smallest mulberries have the most flavor:

> In a culture that claims "bigger is better," it's good to notice how much character can be found in the small, the near, and the accessible.

The softer the berry, the sweeter it usually is:

> We don emotional armor and cultivate strength, but hardness brings with it a certain bitterness.

It takes a lot of roots to hold a tree upright through the heady winds of Spring:

> Family, community, history, tradition, and relationship to place are what keep us grounded in the face of disruption and change. To keep our balance requires as many roots as branches.

Thinking about a previous year's bountiful harvest makes it harder to appreciate what is found on the tree today:

> Dwelling in our minds, in the past or the future, can make it hard to fully taste the fruits of the present.

Mulberry seeds somehow live through the process of being eaten and then passed by birds, and the trees are spread in that way:

> We spread the seeds of insight that survive our lengthy digestion. Those that remain viable are the ones we pass on. And as it is with the birds, we may never get to see what sprouts from them.

Birds and squirrels come from far and wide to feast on the berries, and snakes and owls arrive to feast on them:

> In the hunt for love, it is wise to stay close to that which love seeks.

Some of the tastiest berries can be found lying on the ground:

> Along with the sugar comes a little grit. And while some gifts require we stretch up on tiptoes to receive...the ripest insist we get down on our knees.

There are only mulberries on a wild tree for a short time, and conscientious gatherers will make sure they don't miss it:

> We're each only healthy and savvy for a brief and glorious season. It is thus unwise to allow ourselves to be distracted from the fullest living of life, even for a single day. Nor should we take advantage of its fruitful bounty unless we can give it our complete attention...honor it with our gratitude, and repay it with our acts.

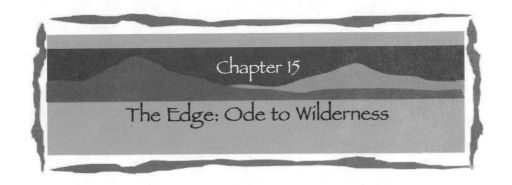

*In the shaman's world, wilderness and the unconscious
become analogous: the one who knows and is at ease in one,
will be at home in the other.*

—Gary Snyder

Wilderness is the vital edge, the point of departure and reentry, the stage and source of magic. Compared to the breathtaking wonderment of the un- chained wilds, rote existence in the dominant paradigm can appear both distracted and deadened. You can see it as the difference between the sparkle in the eyes of a baby, unencumbered by the past or the future, re- sponsive to all that surrounds them, and the vacant pupils of an aging actor, forever lost in the scripts he never wrote, and never experienced. It's the difference between merely existing and fully living, between ignoring our in- stincts and courageously living our dreams.

Wilderness is far more than a legislative designation. And more than virgin meadows and pure streams, although it is the very essence of whole- someness. It is the fundamental combination of land and space, whether harshest desert or unclimbable mountain, which in spite of everything hu- man kind has done to it has somehow maintained the vital capacity of wild- ness. The wilds, like a splash of cold creek water or the unmistakable grunt of a sow bear, have the ability to rush us out of dialogue and into our own creature senses. To stimulate our hearts and get our blood to flow like pow- erful rivers coursing towards sea. To alert us to the necessity of making choices, heeding omens, and pursuing quests. Like sudden fear, joy, or sur- prise, like a narrow escape from death or like root-animal lust, the wilds can so completely fill us with awakeness and a love of life as to leave no room for anything less!

Wilderness is a necessity not a luxury, if for no other reason than this: Too many of our kind, having abandoned the wilds of Nature and the wild in themselves, have increasingly replaced root-experience with intellection and abstraction. Some argue over the details of environmental issues the way they discuss the relative merits of space movies and polyester fashions, football games and facelifts—as if anything in the whole world could mean more than the world itself!

Wilderness is not only magic, it is the very epitome of reality—for nothing is more real than the wild. Nothing as vividly experienced in every sector of one's being. Nothing! It is a spell that awakens, reuniting us with the pleasures of our hearing, our sight, our soul.

So take us, gods and goddesses. Take us, Earth and Spirit. Take us, sweet wildness! Take us outside those walls and limitations we've built around ourselves, the traps of placation and comfort. Precious life is too short! Take us to the edge of the crest, far above the crowd and circumstance below, to where the winds meet in a display of boundless passion. Then let us soak up the wonderment that is our birthright. The wild-seated power that costs us nothing but our illusions and pride. The beauty that costs only our hearts.

Wow! Let amazement fill our pores and ruffle our feathers, like young eagles preparing to ride a stormy updraft. It's at the edge—instructed by place and Spirit, awash in the completeness of the moment, enlivened by possibility—that we become our most authentic and magical selves again.

It is a necessary element in our return to response-able practice and sacred purpose. It is the rain-soaked slickrock on which we chance our destined dance. And it is the edge from which we leap.

Chapter 16

The Sacred Ground

...the moment I felt a connection to the earth, the moment I got grounded, my whole life changed. My surroundings became the path and the path became me.

—Katie Hennessey

You can't really be grounded without stepping outdoors, and walking barefoot on the ground!

—Loba

There are few things more counter-evolutionary than the many trendy philosophies that encourage transcending the body and sailing away from the anchoring planet Earth. This is analogous to the modernist trend of sealing the dead in lead-lined coffins, which are filed above ground in crowded crypts, or the institutional religiosity that posits escape from the cycles and experiences of human existence as some form of salvation. Instead, in New Nature Spirituality, we reconnect and re-pledge to the animal, vegetal, liquid, and mineral greater Self that is sacred Gaia. Indeed, if we are to have any chance of humanity reclaiming a healthy role in the balance of the Whole, we'll need to be as solid inside as rock. And to stick like clay. To be as nutritive as soil. Like a sedimentary deposit, we'll need to settle back into place, serving as food for what grows out of that sacred marriage of hominid and home. And like some lava-tinted igneous formation, we'll need to embody and express the passion of this molten-hearted planet. After centuries of orbiting somewhere above the Earth, outside of our own existence, let it be said that some of us have finally landed.

And what is this land that we bind to and rise from? It is the "sacred ground" that pulses underneath the pavement, breathing deeply through the cracks in the sidewalks and cramped suburban yards. It is the substance of plant and animal and stone, of ancient forms and extincted species reconstituted into the heated soil of the garden and the dirt on our hands. It is the fertile loam that bears our crops, the foundation that supports our dwellings, the geologic extension of our holy Gaian beings. It is the skeletal framework of our destiny, the very *terra firma* of our lives. No wonder when someone makes a unsubstantiated claim we say that it is "groundless"—for without this orb of ground, we'd be nothing but a fleeting formless potential. Without this Earth to manifest through and on, human kind would find itself, quite literally, "lost in space."

It is the most natural and unpretentious people that we call "down to Earth," and it's they who carry in their own inner, fertile fields the wisdom and love of the grounded Whole. And yet we often complain of being "soiled." Like a delusional Lady Macbeth, we try to scrub every last bit of dirt from our bodies, all in the vain hope of washing away the evidence of our organic source, and the reminder of our ultimate earthly destination. But scrub, lie, or hide— we all will die. And until then, live we *must*—not only on, but *for* this special Earthen trust.

It is time for all women and men to stand up for that which we stand upon. There is no more sure measure of the environmental health of the world than the sad depletion and toxification of forest and agricultural soils. There is no greater "common ground" than this, dependent as we are on its mineral purity and organic richness for the foods our burgeoning population eats, and with all of life hanging on the fate of the microbial and fungal communities housed in its top few inches. We need now more than ever a newfound appreciation for the good Queen Dirt—for she is the corporal body of all that has come before, stretched wide and thin like Gaia's sheath or skin...and the promise of what's yet to come. She is part of mineral-Gaia, the beauty of which attracts us to her mountains and parks, her magnetic grid aiding migrating salmon and Southbound larks. Mineral Gaia, who draws down the lightning to both highest peaks and iron seams, and in this manner brought the transformative power of fire to an already dynamic world. She is ever reborn, ever an aspiring adolescent, and yet she's also the oldest gal on the block. Her wind-rounded stones function as an abacus, recording epochs as though seconds, millenniums as moments.

Indeed, it would be accurate to say that all rocks are the "rocks of ages." They are timekeepers and place keepers, speaking from the perspective of eras and eons. In their vibrations are echoes of the tragedies and celebrations that make up evolutionary history, and they align like Easter Island monoliths to point toward the unfolding future. The largest boulders give us a feel for our true, expansive size. The tiny pebbles and fractured shards lying at our feet are some of our own precious bones, waiting once more for a fresh cloaking of flesh. From beach sand to canyon cliffs, we're blessed with an aggregate of teachers, patiently instructing us on the means and ways home.

If we are to remain a distinguishable part of the inspirited Whole, we will have to reawaken a conscious, reciprocal relationship with what is surely *us*: hallowed ground and mineral crust. Do not turn away...but hold onto this rock, this Earth, this way.

It's true what the Aborigines have been telling us: the knowing mountain sighs. This ground is the bridge between our far-reaching dreams, and a reachable sky.

Chapter 17

Sacred Covenants:
Making Pledges to the Places of Power

Many persons have the wrong idea of what constitutes true happiness. It is not attained through self-gratification but through fidelity to a worthy cause.

—Helen Keller

The ancients understood—and we are beginning to recall—the essential reciprocal nature of our relationship to the natural world...and to sacred sites in particular.

With every gift received from a place of power comes an assignment that we can either fail...or fulfill.

The Earthen Spirituality Project at the Sweet Medicine Sanctuary is a place of timeless magic in southwest New Mexico, the "Land of Enchantment." Known as the Gila National Forest, these were the first public wildlands ever set aside for protection—a full 40 years before the passage of the Wilderness Act. The county is more than 80 percent national forest, with miniscule inholdings of private land owned by those seeking one of the last undeveloped mountain ranges in temperate climes. Peaks rise up from ancient seabeds to nearly 12,000 feet in height, laced with streams and spotted with hot springs. Sculpted by the most recent and violent volcanic activity on this continent, the fire colored cliffs climb above pines and oaks, in a river canyon where Geronimo and Victorio once hunted for vision and power. Painted pottery sherds on the ground remind us of a lineage of prayer and caretakership dating back thousands of years. Scattered throughout the sanctuary are the remains of a pit-house village, where the Sweet Medicine (or "Mogollon") People once gathered for instruction and medicine. The rock ledges where my visiting questers sit were polished smooth by the quiet motion of countless yucca sandals, and juniper trees grown out of the center of a ceremonial kiva filled in with rock and earth.

Generation after generation of russet-skinned men and women once made their way down from the headwaters of the two little rivers the Spanish later named the St. Francis and the Tularosa, and ventured up from as far south as the confluence of the Gila in what is now eastern Arizona. Children as well as adults carried baskets of food and offerings on their backs, and other packs were strapped on the camp dogs that followed behind. They came to this special place to honor Solstice and Equinox, to bless plantings and harvests, births and deaths...and to unify and fortify their hearts in the face of what were recurring hard times. They came to ask for insight and clarity, omens and talismans, guidance and visions, blessings and strength. And most importantly, they came to give something back to the land and spirits in return: their attention, focus, devotion, and service. To add their own sweat and stones to its altars, and pledge to its protection. To venerate, consecrate, and celebrate.

We can sense the Sweet Medicine way before we get there. Our normal cognitive processes are gradually derailed as we get nearer to the source of the sanctuary's energies, and intuition and instinct regain their rightful prominence in our whole and holy being. From the area where folks park their vehicles it's a two-mile hike across seven shallow river crossings, like the mythic "seven bridges" on the path to paradise. The canyon narrows at the third of these, making it impossible to proceed any further without getting our feet wet. It's only appropriate that we go shoeless as we cross the holy threshold. It can feel as if we're passing through a porous membrane, alerting us to the presence of power, while simultaneously announcing our arrival to the many spirits of place. The winds usually pick up at this point, tickling the hairs on our skin, inspiring us to reconsider our worthiness, willingness, and preparedness...the purity of our intentions...as well as the degree of our commitment and the depth of our love. Passing this spot on my way to town, it always feels like I'm going the wrong way. As if I were neglecting my duties. As if I were no longer being looked out for. And every time I return, it's not only a coming home...but reunion with an ageless family, a return to my essential work, and the honoring of an irrevocable promise. For more than two decades now, this land has been my teacher and my ally, refuge, and inspiration. It has been the source of both my sensitivity and solace, defining both my purpose and place. And this third juncture has been my portal, my door, my gate.

Becoming the caretaker of such an important site has taught me about the sanctity of all the Earth, even the ground beneath our blanket of concrete and asphalt impositions. But there are a limited number of special places where truths seem far less escapable, illusions less sustainable, and the serendipitous miracles of Gaia more visible and exaggerated. It is them that our ancestors hiked and climbed, with burros and llamas, across ice fields, and under African skies. All of the natural world is magical and precious, needing our guardianship and love, but some areas are host to a greater diversity of plant and animal species. They have more to give in some ways, but are also more sensitive to environmental threats. It's the same with the spiritual landscape: all land is both sacred and inspirited...and yet certain places have higher concentrations of palpable Spirit, where the instructions and energies of the living Earth seem somehow easier to hear, and to feel.

These are the "places of power," arterials we contact whenever we want to get back in touch with the vital pulse of the planet—portals where the effusing energies of a living Earth are clearly more accessible, palatable, and influential. They're revelatory, offering universally applicable wisdom, as well as specific information not available through any other channel, at any other location. They are the energetic locus, the "genius loci," the focal points for the emergence of Spirit in place.

It's true that anyplace can be transformed into a potent sacred site through generations of continuous consecration, focused reverence, maintenance, ceremony, and prayer. Over the years the litany of our oft repeated intentions meld with the echoes of our songs and rites, developing signature energies that can be sensed and tapped by others in times to come. But what I know to be places of power already existed, fully expressed, for eons before any human recognition or use. When altars, temples, and prehistoric villages are found on places of power, it's not the works or attentions of our kind that gives these sites their significance and character. Rather, there have long been seers and geomancers who deliberately sought out potent places for their circles and shrines, identifying them through those ambient energies early Greeks called the "plenum." Such places are often associated with caves, springs, groves, singular mountain peaks, unusual vagaries of geology and topography. But the traditional sites of the Hopi altars are below canyon rims and on the edges of mesas that are seemingly indifferentiable from the landforms surrounding them, and the power of some sites is so strong you can find them in the dark.

One way to be sure about a place of power is by how deeply it affects us. It starts with a perceived invitation in the form of a sign or a feeling, followed by the most intimate exposure and communion. We're usually tested upon arrival, eliciting feelings of dread, and concern that we'll act inappropriately. We may feel as if we're being observed and evaluated. Yet if our minds are quiet and our hearts clear, we are not only accepted but initiated, instructed, and invigorated...emboldened and equipped. A place of power, after all, is where *we* feel more powerful as well.

We're all familiar with Petra and Machu Pichu, Mesa Verde and Stonehenge. But every region, every watershed has its own special spots where the energy is most intense, dreams are most vivid, and visions most alive. As a young pilgrim, I walked through a forest of whispering pines in the Black Hills of South Dakota, basked in the emanations of Mt. Shasta, and snuck past the locked National Park Service gates in order to spend a night in the bowels of Chaco. And now, season after season I am an attendant to this other canyon, the secretive place of Sweet Medicine. I've learned her language well, and translate her insights for all those who are willing to listen.

A volume of water can flood an entire valley with a couple inches of life-sustaining fluid, or concentrate into a solitary channel with enough force to cut through solid rock. We can choose shallow relationships with a multitude of paramours, without taking the time to fully understand or bond with any of them—or we can give all our affection to one or a few individuals, and thereby plumb the very depths of what it means to know and love. In the same way, there is value in traveling to the world's famous sacred sites, garnering what we can, and paying our respects to each. Or we can repeatedly go back to the same site, to the place that calls to us the loudest. It is this way we develop the intimacy of familiars, learn all that the land has to teach, and that we become known to the land. We're inspired to make the most fervent oaths, certain that we'll be returning to keep them. Loyalty leads to trust, as with any relationship. Because it is a relationship we're committed to keep alive, we feel secure investing ourselves and our time. It is this trust and continuity that makes possible the creation and maintenance of shrines, the establishment of ministries and schools, the raising of trees, and the restoration and rewilding of the land. As residents—or as devoted visitor-guardians—we initiate legislative protection, agreements or easements to prevent inappropriate development, despoilment, and destruction. And as a site's impassioned familiars, we're able to channel ceremonies specific to the place we're joined with—those rites that best reflect its character, serving its requirements and desires.

It is such agreement and reciprocity that have made it possible for the Earthen Spirituality Project to be designated a U.S. Fish and Wildlife Service (USFWS) supported wildlife refuge. One hundred and nine years of unrestricted livestock grazing had left the canyon almost barren of vegetation, but thanks to fences and plantings, there's a forest of red willows nearly too dense to walk through today. The endangered willow flycatcher and hundreds of other species of rare birds and mammals make their home in the willows' shade. Cottonwood saplings that were once gobbled up as fast they could take root, are now 30 and 40 feet tall, hosting the nests of ospreys and herons. We've had skunks climb up on our laps, and foxes eat juniper berries in the branches above the kitchen. The mountain lions have returned to scream their lust and hunger, and bear their spotted kits. Sacred objects have been secured away, and the trails of guests and questers pass below spiral petroglyphs marking the infinite cycles of giving and receiving.

Entities and memories commingle in the places where trepidation fuels and destiny rules—gathering busily like children rapt in play. Spirits do not lounge in these environs but strive and aspire, parade and perform. They make an effort to get our attention, waving wildly with leaf-laden arms, trying to flag us out of the stratosphere of our minds and back down to Earth with the flash of white on an elk's rump or the smell of a bear. The muted sounds of ancient laughter and primal drums are not to draw us into the past, but to awaken us to deeper presence...in an always-unfolding present. They implore us to be sentient, connected, compassionate, responsive beings once again. To nourish and manifest our authentic selves, contribute to the well-being and fulfillment of other people and beings, and pledge ourselves to the spirits and places of our enlightenment.

It is one thing to make our way to a place of power, but to be worthy of it's lessons, we must learn to employ them in our everyday lives. We deserve the visions it provides us when we take every risk—and pay any price—to make them real for the world. Our relationship to Spirit requires we take responsibility for those locations where it's housed, concentrated, and made most palpable to the seeker. We honor its blessings not only through acknowledgment and prayer, but by pledging to protect the wholeness, integrity, and intentions of the land. By tending to its spiritual, practical, and ecological needs. By committing to communion and covenant, expression and celebration. By promising a relationship that's attentive, and a love that lasts.

...And by keeping our promises.

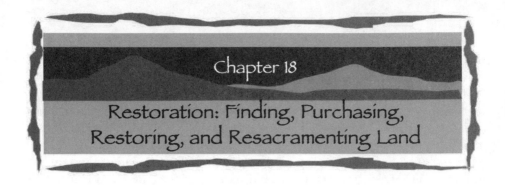

Chapter 18

Restoration: Finding, Purchasing, Restoring, and Resacramenting Land

A society that could heal the dismembered world would recognize the inherent value of each person and of the plant, animal, and elemental life that makes up the earth's living body; it would offer real protection, encourage free expression, and reestablish an ecological balance to be biologically and economically sustainable. Its underlying metaphor would be mystery, the sense of wonder at all that is beyond us and around us, at the forces that sustain our lives and the intricate complexity and beauty of their dance.

—Starhawk

No individual or community exists apart from the land. Even the most insular and distracted populations act out their lives not on a stage but in a place. Ignored, taken for granted, and often covered with a suffocating layer of asphalt and concrete, the area nevertheless continues to exert an influence over the psychologies of the people and the form of their creations: A town's roads are shaped and routed by the local topography; architectural design is partly a response to the predominate weather patterns; and the characteristic temperament of a region's inhabitants is to some degree sculpted by the hand...of the land. The conservative independence fostered by life in Northern Canada and Alaska, the austerity and simplicity of plains dwellers, the laconic sensuality of the steaming Southwest.

This is all the more true for the most sensitive of our kind, the solitary seeker, and the greater spiritual and Pagan communities. Not only are the individuals more aware of the influence and needs of the land, but also the ways they are informed and inspired by the spirits of place. And increasingly they are recognizing the need for a reciprocal, promissory relationship with the land.

Only a relatively few spiritual or magical communities actually live together, and its members are likely living scattered throughout the city—but increasingly, groups have been combining their resources to purchase property out of town where they can gather for ritual and prayer, personal healing, and communal celebration. For those involved in New Nature Spirituality, securing, rewilding, and resacramenting a piece of property both grounds and manifests our values and beliefs. And the restoring of even a small piece of land to its original natural state does more than perhaps anything else to help restore the health and wholeness of our personal selves and magical communities. The time is right to not only go out and experience inspirited Nature, but also to make a commitment to conserve, nourish, heal, and honor it.

Finding "the Place"

The price of fertile farmland is going up, and a 20-acre homestead within driving distance of a city or school can cost a mint. On the other hand, the properties that are the best candidates for wildlands restoration are likely priced much less. Such prime pieces are often isolated, with unmaintained access roads or no roads at all, which also makes them ideal for events and gatherings that are best kept private. They may be too marshy for development, but be perfect for re-creating a bird-loving wetland. Or the property could be a narrow canyon that's half floodplain, and the other half "unusable" rocky terrain—as our land was first described!

Of course it was this very "undesirability" that attracted us to what became the premier wildlife sanctuary in this region. Our property is located on a gorgeous bend of the river they named after St. Francis, seven Jeep-sinking crossings from the nearest pavement in southwest New Mexico. The county is more than 80 percent national forest, with miniscule inholdings of private land owned by those seeking one of the last undeveloped mountain ranges in temperate climes. Nearby is the Gila, millions of acres of public wildlands set aside for protection a full 40 years before the passage of the Wilderness Act.

Fencing and Restoration

We arrived to find that 109 years of unrestricted cattle grazing had left the canyon nearly barren of green. There were hardwoods and ponderosas, of course, as well as a dozen varieties of cacti, but there were no grasses or wildflowers. Many of the magnificent old cottonwoods were gone, washed away by erosion-caused floods, and any willow or cottonwood saplings sprouting up to replace the toppled giants were quickly eaten by the hungry cows. Public land in the Southwest is a hard place for livestock, and unless managed closely, they'll tend to congregate along the few rivers and streams, trampling what they don't consume. The damage here was done years before there was any such thing as "holistic range management," where herds are moved often in order to give the vegetation time to grow back. For this fragile riparian ecosystem, the obvious first step was to keep any free ranging cattle out with effective and well-maintained fences.

Our property is an inholding surrounded on all sides by national forest. The last thing we wanted to do when we got here was to stretch barbed wire across an unmarked landscape, but we could see the potential value in it. The proof, as they say, is "in the pudding": after 11 years of being fenced off, we now have a dense forest of red willows, offering shelter to the federally endangered willow flycatcher and hundreds of other species of rare birds and mammals. Young cottonwoods are already 30 to 40 feet tall, and are host to poised kingfishers, roosting herons, and nesting ospreys. Wild skunks sometimes climb up on our laps for handouts, and foxes munch on juniper berries in the branches above a primitive outdoor kitchen. Bear have moved back in, and for the last five years a pair of mountain lions have felt safe enough to return and raise their spotted kits.

Assistance with the cost of the fence came from the USFWS, through its innovative Partnerships in Wildlife program. Anyone can apply for the limited program, by demonstrating his or her commitment to restoring a piece of land, and by promising to maintain it in part as habitat for waterfowl or other foraging wildlife. The USFWS also helped cover the costs of our first tree plantings, and soon the warm months were given over to revegitating the canyon with long-missing native species. The red willow was some of the first to make a comeback, with an extensive and untouched root system soon propelling new growth skyward. To hasten their comeback and to fortify the bare riverbanks against the floods, we carefully cut branches from the established bushes and stuck them at intervals in the damp ground. Rare wild grapes planted at the base of shading trees quickly spread out their bounty of tasty leaves and delicious fruit. Wildflower seeds gathered in Fall were planted by poking a hole in the ground with a sharpened stick, barely bending over to drop two kernels in each waiting womb.

Going Native

One of the first things we did was to research what species of plants and animals live on or near the property now, and which have been recently forced out. The hardest part was determining which species belonged, or at least "got along"—and which were highly destructive invaders. Some of the exotics we catalogued came across the Bering Straits with the first human arrivals to the Americas. Soft and fuzzy mullein, while not indigenous, doesn't seem to outcompete. But others, such as aromatic horehound and the beautiful tamarisk tree quickly colonize and dominate any riparian area they sail into, forcing out many of the native populations. Like conquistadors, these botanical opportunists are adept at making the transition from guest to master!

The most noticeable incursion was the horehound, its seeds hitchhiking up onto the mesa stuck to our socks, and moving through the rest of the county in the tails of horses and the alfalfa hay they eat. It's an attractive plant, famous for its use in sweet cough drops, and is hardy enough to sprout in hard barren ground. At first we welcomed it, but it wasn't long before it formed a solid crusty plane of yard-high vegetation too thick to walk through. Where the areas around our cabin and below the cliffs were once graced by desert mariposa and beeweed, soon there was only horehound. Prickly-poppy and evening primrose, nettle and mallow, fishhook cactus and fleabane were being eased out of their own neighborhoods in the vegetal equivalent of a hostile takeover bid. It was hard accepting the hands-on responsibility of re-moving them, one plant at a time, feeling for them as we made room for natives again.

The tamarisk is another invader, and it wasn't too many years before we started spotting their pretty pink blossoms as they made their way into the canyon. These European salt cedars pose no great threat to their home turfs, but once released into North America, they were soon the only tree to be found along many of the rivers of the Southwest. Fast growing and herbicide resistant, they produce a shower of mineral salts that make the soil inhospi-table to any competing shoots. Without resistance, they soon smother the willows and immature cottonwoods. Digging them up by hand was labor-intensive but necessary, because if even a foot or two of root is left in place, it can grow an entire new tree!

The counterpart to the tamarisk in the Southeast is the kudzu vine, which once having escaped its ornamental plots in the suburbs, is now fast becom-ing the dominant species, climbing and eventually choking the standing trees. And it's not only a problem with plants but with animals. Rabbits released into Australia as a meat source quickly took over and decimated the vegeta-tion. Sailing vessels acted as arks for the emigration of the Norwegian rat, which, along with the mongoose imported to control them, has wiped out hundreds of species unique to the Hawaiian Islands. Zebra mussels have hitch-hiked into the Great Lakes inside the ballast of commercial ships, and now threaten an entire fishery.

Seeds and Trails

I arrived here thinking this dry, usually hard ground was particularly du-rable, and never considered limiting our pedestrian traffic to trails. Only as the paths to certain places took shape on their own did I come to realize how much greener, how much more alive it was wherever we *didn't* walk.

As a kid I was known to duck under the railings at parks and exhibitions in search of my own direction, and for most of my life I've balked at guided tours and marked trails, so it was with some trepidation that I arranged the first of hundreds of surface rocks into borders channeling our footfall. I took them from a wide area so as not to disrupt the appearance of the land.

While carrying the rocks, they became more personal for me, each with its own unique shape and color. Some were relatively light and porous, while others were dense and heavy. Crystal glinted in some of the chunks of lava like a star nursery. Round black rock was found nestling inside a matrix of white sandstone, and ruddy aggregate hosted the greatest colonies of lichen.

And here was yet another lesson in sensitivity: take care to set the stones down *lichen-side up*. Actually miniature forests made up of millions of microscopic individuals, it takes lichen centuries to reduce a rock to soil, gumming the minerals, drinking in the sun: lime green lichen, burnt orange lichen, rock eatin' lichen. Soon the rock borders are catching any eroding soil. Like the stone check-dams laid across every arroyo and drainage, they serve as slightly raised seedbeds for a progression of wild blossoms, one native species after the next taking it's seasonal turn in the light.

As much as I can resent restrictions, we soon saw the importance of limiting our impact in other ways as well. Nesting bald eagles moved out of their colored cliffs when we rode in with a loud vehicle, and only returned to the canyon when things quieted back down. We made the difficult decision not to have pets on the sanctuary, and immediately began noticing how much closer the deer and coatimundi, the birds and lizards would come to us. Binding land use covenants were signed and entered into the courthouse records that put a cap on the amount of people who could live here, while specifying the number and type of structures that could be built.

To avoid coming into conflict with the wildlife we were attracting, we chose to forego a domestic garden. The surprising benefit was the large variety of indigenous foods that now flourish naturally here, including tasty nettles, coletus (lamb's quarters), acorns, black walnut, cattail, currant, mulberry, grape, and prickly pear, to name a few. Wild foods are yummy and require no watering, weeding, or battling with hungry insects, raccoons, or javelina!

The Wild Covenant

When talking about what makes something "wild," it helps to understand its true meaning: not "wild" as in "destructive, out of control," but as in "willful" and "true to its own nature." Restorationists are dedicated to healing and protecting the integrity—the natural wholeness—of a property, an ecosystem, or an entire bioregion.

It's great to keep some places completely free of human habitation, but it can also benefit a restoration project to have caretakers on site at all times. One way to monitor the threats and record the improvements is to live in intimate contact with the land one season after the next, one year after another. Or barring that, we can make a pledge to visit the land every other weekend, keeping an inventory of its life forms, and doing the roll-up-the-sleeves work needed to bring it back into its natural glory.

This is the wild covenant, a set of commitments, and our willful follow-through.

Practica

Finding, dedicating, and restoring land is no easy project, and I offer the following practical as well as visionary suggestions:

- ◉ Make purchasing and restoring ceremonial land a part of your spiritual and magical practice. Seek out others in your community to share the responsibilities and cost of the purchase. Enlist folks with a knowledge of legal affairs, conservation biology, and geomancy. But be willing to do extra or even unpleasant jobs in order to pay for the land, and sacrifice other activities and priorities you enjoy in order to make it happen, with or with out the help of others.

- ◉ Look for property conducive to group/ritual privacy and wildlands restoration, the more isolated and less commercially desirable, the better. The longer the place has sat unwanted on the real estate market, the more likely you are to get both a good price, and generous terms. Look especially for parcels that border existing wildlife refuges, state lands, "green belts," or national forest on one or more sides. If you already own rural property, consider setting aside a portion of it for the specific purpose of rewilding and resacramenting. If you can't afford any property at all, consider contacting both absentee landowners (their addresses are recorded at the courthouse in every county) and existing conservation trusts about letting you volunteer with the restoring of some parcel.

- ◉ Define the principles, values, and aesthetics of "wild" and "sacred." Research what the land you commit to looked like before any substantial human impact (such as development, logging, or livestock grazing). Research ancient (indigenous) use of the land, and the place-based beliefs of these people.

- ◉ Remove any modern human artifacts, garbage, etc. Make any residential or event structures as beautiful as possible, using natural materials that blend with the character of the land.

- ◉ Do as comprehensive a biological survey as you can to determine what plants and animals exist there now. Find out which plants and animals are indigenous and which are exotic invaders. Determine which of the exotics are destructive or outcompete the natives. Manage for diversity, encouraging the widest possible variety of indigenous life-forms. Remove destructive invader species when possible: pulling the plants by hand, fencing out livestock, live trapping and transporting feral cats, etc. Attract the native wildlife by providing them with sources of water (where none exists already), forage, and shelter. Wildflowers invite insects, which attract lizards and birds, followed by the ringtailed cat and gray fox. Planting wild grape and plum helps bring in the deer and elk, and sometimes the lion who feed on the deer and elk follow. Actively spread the seeds and transplant the saplings of rare native species, and reintroduce those that are missing. Identify which of these plant species serve as the best source of forage for the area's wildlife, and make them a priority.

◉ Pick places for rituals, shrines, group circles, camping, etc. Restrict activity near springs or other fragile environments. To direct foot traffic, plan trails where needed, and line the edges with rocks or fallen logs. By building trails as much as possible perpendicular to the high ground, their borders act as ideal seedbeds, and as a check on erosion. Limit resident and visitor impact, with covenants restricting activities and noise levels, such as vehicle use. Keep in mind the designs of Spirit, the integrity of the landforms, and the well-being of the wildlife whenever making lifestyle or land use decisions.

◉ Draw up a clear statement of intention and purpose, and incorporate it in any protective covenants, or in the mission statement of your church or conservation trust.

Securing Land and Dedicating Use

There are several strategies for improving the odds your prime piece of wildlife habitat, group gatherings, and spiritual contemplation won't some-day be leveled for another condominium or amusement park:

◉ Land covenants are land use restrictions between buyers and sellers, or between partners. They're attached to the property deed, and are recorded at the local county courthouse. Problem: Covenants are too often overturned by high-paid lawyers.

◉ A conservation easement is a type of self-zoning, where you guarantee some land use activities and prohibit others, by signing away certain landowner "rights" to a monitoring and enforcing agency (try approaching local land trusts, as well as the U.S. Forest Service). There are easements guaranteeing property will never be logged, or that it will always be reserved for agriculture, or that it will remain wild for all time. Problem: It can be difficult finding someone to accept the responsibility for the easement unless you're also donating a sizable "maintenance fund."

⊚ Conservation trusts are another level of protection, where you either donate or will your property to an existing trust, or else set up your own. A trust is a nonprofit corporation with a charter that defines the uses of the land it owns or controls. Problems: Starting and keeping your own trust going can be a lot of work, even for a cooperating neighborhood group. And if you sign your property over to an existing conservancy, you can't always "trust" that they won't sell or trade it for other sensitive land on down the line.

⊚ Education, commitment, and lineage may be the most important protective mechanism of all. It's essential we educate ourselves, our community, and our heirs in both the lessons of Nature and the needs of the land.

Outreach

No project can exist apart from the larger community, and every restored wildland has something special to teach those who come to feel, and to heal. As a result, we soon began hosting workshops and other educational programs at the sanctuary, eventually launching a Website to broaden our outreach, and self-publishing books filled with our insights and experiences. As the Earthen Spirituality Project, we've brought in students and interns from around the world, teaching them not only the philosophy and practice of restoration but also awareness and responsibility, the art of reading animal tracks, and the gathering and preparing of indigenous foods. They learn how to open to the gifts and instructions of the natural world, and to give the most of themselves in exchange.

Developing a relationship with a particular piece of land serves both the Earth and the people who love and commit to her. Securing habitat for indigenous plants and animals ensures that we, too, will always have places where we can feel more native, more at peace, more alive. Doing whatever it takes to purchase, rewild, and restore a piece of sacred Gaia makes us worthy of her blessings...while in turn, restoring both our magical community, and our most magical selves.

Chapter 19

Coming Closer: Animal Teachers and the Legacy of the Overlooked

I have found animals in me when I stroll in the forest.
I hesitate before a large dragonfly, I step
like a cat in the night, I have felt something
lift along my neck
when a wolf howls.

—Loren Eisley

There are many ways of re-becoming our true selves...in deep relationship to Spirit and place. And there are plenty of willing teachers and worthy role models. Of these, there are perhaps no better examples or inspirations than the plants and animals inhabiting each Earthen bioregion: the coyotes and raccoons of alleyways, the wolves of unbroken wilderness, and the leviathans of the deep. And not only defiant eagles, but also the plainest looking local fowl, which create homes within the solid promise of hollow street signs. They're each an accessible and instructive component of creation. They are our teachers...and at the point of wholeness/holiness, they are us.

In today's modern society, the tendency is to view the entire rest of the living world from afar—whether through the eyepiece of a researcher's microscope or the lens of the video camera. We've increasingly become witnesses rather than participants, studying Nature more than we actually observe it, and observing it more than interacting with it. Our beloved domestic pets, glossy postcards, and televised "nature shows" have become the primary locus of interface between civilized human kind and the nonhuman world. Our understandings are largely mental—and thus superficial. We may be vaguely disappointed when the place where we vacation doesn't look quite as magnificent as it did on the picture calendar. We take note of what we consider to be the most "scenic" vistas, voting to set some of these aside as national parks, monuments, or designated wilderness areas. We've consequently neglected the fruitful wetlands, the ecologically important bogs and fragile deserts...and the wide and "plain" spaces between, essential as both buffer zones and wildlife habit.

What is this joy? That no animal
falters, but knows what it must do?
That the snake has no blemish,
that the rabbit inspects his strange surroundings
in white star-silence?

.   .   .   .

Those who were sacred have remained so,

.   .   .   .   .

...only the sight that saw it
faltered and turned from it.

(Denise Levertov, "Come into animal presence")

We've been trained in this culture to fear intimacy and cultivate objectivity, so it's no wonder we're quick to acknowledge the grandeur of the coastal redwoods, and yet hardly notice the quiet beauty of the California broadleaf sage. Or that we fail to protect that fast disappearing sage from encroaching suburban sprawl, but at times organize or sign petitions to preserve the giant red-hued trees. It's no surprise that when asked to name a familiar wild animal, people will tend to cite the largest, flashiest, or most celebrated, such as bears, hawks, and wolves. Or that the most visible campaigns to save threatened species have focused on the highly symbolic bald eagles, cuddly pandas, and behemoth whales.

As we all know, the very fabric of biological diversity is at stake, the state of ecological balance, and even the continuation of inspirited evolution itself. These things hinge not only on the black rhinoceros and extirpated grizzly, but also on communities of sickened plankton and coral under siege, on the lesser kangaroo rat and the red willow flycatcher, the quickly disappearing honey bees and glad croaking frogs. To some degree, the smaller the lifeform, the more irreplaceable its species' functions are. If the eagle were to go extinct today, other creatures would more or less fulfill it's role as hunter scavenger. But if, for example, we were to lose the many kinds of mychorrizal fungi—now threading their way through the hallowed ground of this world like lace—it could be disastrous for the whole of terrestrial life. If you think about it, butterflies and ants are each crucial to the health of the forest, and the microbes that break organic matter down into soil may be the most essential of them all.

The effect of our "disconnect" is clearly personal as well as ecological, spiritual as well as physical. Our ignorance of the microflora and microfauna potentially diminishes us as well as it does them. We're impoverished by our distance from the swirling muses of bird flight, and the sage advice of the meadow mice. The "insignificant" wren offers up lessons of familial devotion and joy in the face of every circumstance. The hummingbird speaks to the issue of death in rebirth with its penchant to rise out of a torpor brought on by fright like Jesus from the tomb. The smallest snake can teach honesty and trust. The "noncharismatic" challenge our level of awareness and capacity for gratitude. The unappealing species test our concepts of beauty, while the uncuddly stretch our ability to embrace and love. And every diverse form of life affirms in us—the redemptive faith in miracles!

The overlooked and derided are a part of our constituency, as is all of creation. Each contributes their lineage to the influences that shaped us. We evolved with them as part of this mysterious Godly purpose, and we thus reflect and embody them all. They are the plant and animal context, from which our kind arose. They are our sustenance and inspiration, our teachers and totems, our companions and guides. And they, every one of them, are the forces that helped to define us as human.

There is certainly no more stunning image than those now famous photographs of the Earth poised against the blackness of space. More than anything else, those images give us a picture of how finite and even fragile our blue planet really is. And yet to really "make sense" of the natural world, we need to be close enough to employ our underused senses...to touch and smell and taste it! We might be better off focusing on a single continent rather than the entire globe—on a particular bioregion, a specific mountain range, a recognizable canyon, a certain bend in the stream, some exact spot next to familiar sparkling water. Indeed, we can only know the land one rock at a time, at the point where our sensate bodies make contact with the breathing, birthing ground.

All true understanding comes not so much from information as from *relationship*. In fact, the more intimate this relationship, the deeper our understanding. It is the same, whether we're talking about a planet or a lover: we learn through the processes of interaction and reciprocity. We're informed through our corporal, emotional, and spiritual familiarity with the fine details and subtle nuances of the "other." We come to recognize every attractive mole on the loved one's body, and notice every rash that might threaten it. We become familiar with the sound their breath makes when they're gently asleep, notice how it quickens in honest fear or creature lust, and worry when it grows shallow in illness or silent in death. We discover and attend to our lover's rarest and least obvious qualities, while reveling in the familiarity—and universality—of the common and mundane. In the same way we learn to acknowledge every sweet new bud that appears on our houseplants, and to tune into the signs that signal their contentment or trauma. We may also come to notice any evidence of distress in the creek we spend weekend after weekend playing in, grateful for every endangered bird, conscious of every common bug and bubble!

We do not live "on" this Earth so much as with and within it. In conscious, intimate relationship, we're thrust back into the immortal world beyond separation, into the place where magic and the mundane are one. We recognize how, like the bison and the gnat, we *too* belong. We remember ourselves not as visitors on some strange and hostile landscape, but as the residents and extensions of this Spirit-filled All. We come to experience in our hearts and bones, our bodies and our souls, the reality of our connective beingness.

We're enjoined through our attention to the small as well as the large, the vast as the nearly indiscernible. The simple rituals of listening to the neighborhood trees or harvesting dandelions from the yard, in our observance of our amazing brethren insects or acceptance of the rodents in the wall, we're initiated back into the fold. We realize once again that this is our *home*—the immensity of our re-forming text and flesh, the resurfacing of our eternal spirits—and how every tiny part and particle is another vital element in its completeness. We experience ourselves as but a single cell of a corporal planet, and our planet as a cell making up the greater body of a holy unlimited universe.

Chapter 20

Lessons of the Furry Buddhas

It is easier to produce ten volumes of philosophical writings
than to put one principle into practice.

—Leo Tolstoy

The thing that astonished him was that cats should have two
holes cut in their coat exactly at the place where their eyes are.

—G.C. Lichtenberg

In the two decades that I've taught here in this enchanted New Mexico canyon, I've often been asked "which teachings" I follow, or which "mentors" influenced my rather eclectic way of sharing the secrets of the living world. The truth is, I follow my instincts and intuition more than any known practice, though I've discovered truths common to them all, but much of who I am and most of what I've authored has grown out of the immediate lessons of Nature and direct interaction with the inspirited Earth. Like many others, I've been transformed by the examples set by faint or swelling rivers, the behavior of the beasts, the rootedness of plants, the parable of a fallen swallow...and the awareness and playfulness of the North American bobcat.

Perhaps no creature makes a better role model than these spotted "furry Buddhas," licentiously advertising their lust and hunger in wild howls and mad scratchings. Their tracks constitute a veritable bible of awareness, full of passages describing warrens and rat holes, concealment and honesty, frivolity and fight, feathers and flight! They are like four-legged alchemists, converting life into death, and death into life: avatars of perfect cyclic beingness!

I've recently had the pleasure of getting to know one particularly long-legged female. She is but the latest in a long line of backwoods cats to call this wildlife sanctuary home, her personal habits and transferable lessons each dutifully recorded by the man-who-writes. Like those other venerable citizens of the wilder realms, she embodies a holy joy we'd do well to emulate, and an ageless wisdom we too can share.

I believe the time is ripe for enlightenment! The portals of canyon and forest swing wide at our approach, and every wishing star aligns. Go ahead, don't be shy! Approach the set of fresh imprints made by the Master's fuzzy feet, and press your forehead to the giving ground. Her instructions for a satisfying and honorable life are simple, and I feel privileged to translate as follows:

> The world is a magical place...and you are one magical cat!
>
> Risk discomfort for the sake of adventure.
>
> Live as if there's no such thing as the future, because there really isn't.
>
> Inject into the present, conscious moment only the most precious of memories, and those essential to your survival.
>
> Direction is important. Whenever you're not making moves to avoid something, make sure that you're moving with a destination or result in mind.
>
> When you want to be seen, make a grand show of it! Otherwise, lay low and observe the world unfolding around you.
>
> All the world is a book. Take time to read it.
>
> All things in the world fall into two categories: benefits and threats—and sometimes they can be both. Survival depends on knowing which is which. Wisdom is a matter of acting accordingly.
>
> You can hear best when you are still.
>
> The quietest among us invariably stalk barefoot.
>
> The nose knows.
>
> When smelling for trouble, don't forget to smell the flowers too.

To be wild is to be "willed": true to our authentic needs and nature. Never pretend to be anything but what you are.

The tamed are at a distinct disadvantage. "Domesticated" means "with deadened senses."

The longer the hunt, the stronger the legs. The more difficult the trail, the stronger the will.

Just because it isn't easy doesn't mean it's not the right thing to do. We have to chance getting stickers in our tongue if we want to get the burrs out of our feet.

For every single step that you take, look around twice.

Self-respect is a prerequisite to earning the respect of others.

Anytime you're not actively being pursued, don't bother being afraid.

When outnumbered, retreat. When outnumbered and cornered, go down fighting.

Better to chew off your own foot than get trapped in an unhealthy situation.

Know that Hell is confinement, no matter how benign, and that Heaven is the knowledge of oneness that comes without words on a full moon night.

Automobiles are far more dangerous than guns.

Avoid roadkills: an easy meal often comes at a high price, and "convenient" is another way of saying "in close proximity to a substantial threat."

When possible, pick dens and situations with more than one exit.

Foresight is the application of past experience, ancient instinct, and the immediate enlivened senses.

Once you know what you want, pursue it.

Happiness is purpose. Purpose is a clear goal and a hot trail.

There's no doubt a lure can attract game, but the best hunters have no use for deceit.

Shed all extra clothing in the Summer, then bundle up for the Winter's cold.

Don't waste your time thinking, when you could be deeply feeling instead.

Real satisfaction comes from living close to the land, close to the ground.

Finding a mate depends as much on where you are as who you are.

Sexual attraction is more sense of smell than common sense.

The best sex isn't always the most gentle.

The best way to get your mate to lick you is to start licking and preening your mate.

Be extra wary among strangers, and extra cuddly with family and friends.

Never fake affection.

If your friends won't rub your back, then rub your back on your friends.

Make sweet noises whenever something feels good. Purr to indicate you're happy.

Always play with your food.

There are many more mice caught than turkeys. Accomplishing something big is reason to feel proud, but it's our many little accomplishments that sustain us.

Life is a meal to be enjoyed. Gorge yourself whenever possible, and store what you can. When between feasts, don't whine about it.

Make up for eating so much by running up and down trees.

Explore the ordinary as though it were infinitely fascinating...because it is!

Don't let a single butterfly go by unnoticed.

Maintain your dignity, even when acting as silly as you feel.

And whenever you are not busy playing with your food, running up and down trees, or rubbing your back on your friends...curl up in a safe place and sleep.

When death finally overtakes you, make sure it finds you fully, wholly alive.

While seemingly unattached to outcome, the Master wishes us well.

Chapter 21

Tracking Magic: Tools of Enchantment, Practices for Paying Attention

When I close my eyes, I see trails: ones I glanced at and never
followed, some minutes old, others faded by sun and wind;
trails that led me to some momentary brightness; many that led
nowhere at all. Today, if I travel out, there will be more, all
holding out a question, a promise of life somewhere ahead.

—Nick Jans

There's a kind of awareness housed not in mind and thought, but in flesh and bone. It is the way of the spiritual warrior, the conscious magician, the primitive hunter, and the animal within. It bypasses language and logic, plunges us back into our ancient animal senses and the vital, present moment. It's an enchanted and awakened state sometimes accessed through meditation, summoned forth by the onset of love, and triggered by the proximity of real or imagined dangers...like a near miss in traffic, or a rattle from under the sagebrush! Or the imminent presence of a 180-pound throat-crushing mountain lion, equipped by evolution with a decided advantage over thinner-skinned prey such as straggling deer...and struggling writers.

I'd been following the tracks for hours, sometimes getting so close that I could smell her. Unarmed, I watched as a set of streamside paw marks gradually filled with water, and saw the grass where she'd so recently stepped slowly springing back in homage to the Summer sun. Granted, I was comforted knowing lions are in more danger from humans than we are from them, and that most of the few cougar attacks involve decrepit or inexperienced cats leaping on joggers mistaken for Walkman-wearing rabbits. Nonetheless, it takes but a single glimpse of claw marks 6 feet up a tree to awaken anyone's atrophied sensorium. And the perks of the awakening are immediate: the nose that smells for cat is more inclined to discern the scent of the various wildflowers. Eyes on the lookout for cat signs are sure to notice the microcosms of twisted root and bejeweled insect life unfolding at our feet, or the animate shapes clouds make in local turquoise skies.

Tracks are stories written in hoof and claw, mud and sand. A spot in the snow ruffled by feathers and spotted with blood tells of a hawk's felling of a cottontail rabbit. Other marks speak of curiosity and courtship, and of fully lived lives. When we fail to notice these subtle signs and telltale indications is when we're most likely to find ourselves "off track." In fact, tracking can be both a measure of and a cure for "cluelessness." For our ancestors, the ability to "read track" could mean the difference between starvation and a mess of jerky drying on pine bough racks...between us catching a dinner seal, and ending up some frisky grizzly's meal. For us contemporary folk it can still be a way to sharpen our senses, raising our awareness of the details and clues of the real world around us. Getting home from a day on the trail, we can't help but notice how much sweeter music sounds to our freshened ears. Eyes taught to discern the minutia of sign are better able to appreciate the thoughtful elements of a psychedelic painting. Noses stirred by the subtle smells of the forest come back ripe for the scent of a lover or a kitchen's characteristic bouquet.

It was nearly dusk when I finally turned around, heading home the very same way that I'd come. I saw them, just as I began slipping into an out-of-body preoccupation with events past, with impending dinners and beckoning hot tubs. There, on top of my own fresh boot prints appeared a distinct set of tracks for me to see—proof that the lion had, in turn, followed me!

In conscious tracking, every turn in the trail is like the turning of a page. The universe is seen rich with impressions, imbued with not only lyric beauty, but a message, a moral, a purpose. We do not need to go far for the experience, when little miracles are afoot in every backyard and park.

Sign is a kind of enchantment or sorcery in that it can help lead us deeper into the experience of Wonderland, and in the process, deeper into our own enchanted beings. Its mindful practice encourages our reimmersion in the here and now, in the close-at-hand world of instinct and intuition, sensation and response. Instructors of this fine art sometimes refer to it as the "Zen of tracking": a great waking up—both to our enlivened selves—and to the always-waking world of which we're an integral part.

Tracking self. Tracking life. Tracking magic.

Chapter 22

Earth Changes

O Ha Le
O Ha Le
I am waiting for the change.

—Geronimo's death song

She is finding ways to love her mother. She is finding how to
love through the natural disaster.

—Loba

The Earth is a magical set of processes...and a tumultuous cauldron, forever subject to cycles of natural stress and catastrophe. Some mountain ranges were midwifed by a great and tremulous uplift, and others by a fearsome volcanic surge...and it's thanks to their gradual crumbling that we're provided both sand and soil. The arrival of new life forms has often signaled the disappearance of others, throughout the long history of this Gaian Earth Mother. It is nonetheless difficult to name a period in time when there's ever been this diversity of natural and manmade disasters, occurring either simultaneously or in such rapid succession.

Most alarming is the current acceleration of events that are affecting the entire world. Including interpersonal violence and political repression—the destruction of the World Trade Center and the wars the event has inspired. A surge in gang killings and wife beatings. An increase in authoritative government and the abrogation of civil liberties and civil rights. Systematic religious, racial, and cultural genocide. And also financial disruption: international stock market volatility, and an imploding of the economies of Russia, South America, and Southeast Asia leading to starvation and social unrest. Along with greater health risks and epidemics: the spread of cancer, AIDS, acute environmental sensitivities, food allergies, psoriasis and heart disease, rampant alcoholism and prescription drug abuse. Plus the ecological crisis: burgeoning overpopulation, and a dominant global culture promoting illusion and distraction. The infestation of the Great Lakes with zebra mussels, and the drying up of Lake Baikal in Siberia. PCBs (polychlorinated biphenyls) in the water resulting in hermaphrodite polar bears. Toxic herbicides and pesticides impacting depleted croplands, the wiping out of ecologically essential predators, and the clear-cutting of fragile rainforest ecosystems. The disappearance of frog and amphibian species worldwide, and the genetic manipulation of animals and plants. Plus the polluting of the air, and unrepentant destruction of the ozone layer. Killer bees, and the over-fishing of the seas....

Then there are those mounting conflagrations that are not as easy to attribute to a single act or oversight. Relief agencies around the world report they've never been spread so thin, attempting to alleviate one humanitarian disaster after another. The Antarctic ice shelf is breaking up, hurricanes are on the increase, and a season of famine in Africa is all too often followed by another. As I write this, the American West is in the fifth year of record drought, a chronic condition only slightly alleviated by the Winter's gracious rains. We've been beset by ever-larger forest fires, and deadly bark beetles have infested many of the remaining stands. The famous Rio Grande is running at a fraction of its normal volume, while the Southeast has nearly been washed away by record-breaking floods. It's as if Earth and Spirit were jumping up and down, getting ever louder and more shrill in the effort to grab our attention. And indeed, they are! The rustling leaves of the trees beckon us to notice their beauty and grace, before the Autumn reckoning when each tumbles from its sylvan place. Similarly, tragedies call on us to wake up...and personally tend to their needs, roots, and causes before it's too late.

There are potential consequences should our kind not heed the imploring of the existing Shamans and elders, as well as the dire portents of our communicative world. They are reflected in the oft foretold fall of Babylon, in the prayers of the Tibetans, and the prophecies of the Hopi. In the nuclear storms of the dark gods Tezcatlipoca and Huitzilopochtli, the promise of Quetzalcoatl, and the Viking legend of Ragnarok: human kind—systematically disenfranchised from sacred self, Earth, and Spirit—could pay an unnecessarily tragic price.

Note that paying a price isn't the same as either penalty or penance, it's simply a matter of responsibility: the portentous results of our collective failure to respond. Contrary to certain social and religious dictums, we're being neither tested nor punished. More accurately, the directive inspirited Earth is probing for new healing, for new ways of being and relationship that can return the Whole to balance. She's probing for those precious empathics who can hear her cries, sense her needs, and feel her cumulative pain. And she's probing for a reaction, as if to ask, "Is anyone home? Does anyone notice? Does anyone care?"

The significance of the Earth changes is so great and the social condition so urgent, it's tempting to reject the implications and duck the assignment. It's certainly simpler to blame it all on the power of evil spirits, the manipulations of scheming extraterrestrials, the trickery of a hellish devil, the retribution of a wrathful God...or on an impervious corporate state. It's a relief on some level to imagine that the forces of destruction are insurmountable, the perpetrators too powerful for us to bother attempting to intervene. But whenever there is a human or institutional cause, we share a degree of culpability, and we find both an opening for activism and a chance for reformation. And when the tumult and tragedy are set into motion by something bigger than our mortal hominid kind, we can still assume we have a part to play...contributing both to the creation of the imbalance itself, and to the global healing that must follow.

We were each born with a body that regulates its internal hungers and heat, triggers the urge to reproduce, and heals its cuts and wounds. A bodily fever is a valuable curative response to a dangerous infection. While a fever can potentially kill the patient as well as the disease, it's not some dark force that's out to get us. In a similar manner, violent earthquakes and viral outbreaks function as a terrestrial fever that indicates, and can sometimes help eliminate, the imbalance and dis-ease threatening the corporal Earthen body. We, too, are integral elements and agents of planetary being, planetary change, and we have the daily *informed* choice of being either part of the problem or part of the cure. Ignorance is not a lack of information; it's deliberately ignoring the impact of our lifestyles, the results of both what we've done, and what we have so far failed to do. Ignoring the hushed screams of falling old-growth forests, and of the hundreds of species yearly banished into extinction. Ignoring the pleas of motherless children, abused wives, and those hungry homeless camped on our streets. Ignoring the preeminent mission of our kind and times, which is to reconnect, re-member, resacrament, and restore.

While in some ways it's the more difficult path, being a servant of Gaian truth and Gaian healing has some immediate and lasting rewards. So much of this work involves reinhabiting our animal bodies and the vital present moment, where we can fully experience with every one of our six senses the unfolding world around us. It is here we discover not only problems and challenges but their benefits and solutions. Here we notice the taste of our meals and savor the scent of our lovers. When we plant seeds or saplings, we plant ourselves in place and time. Every circle we cast, every ritual we practice or invent creates a magic that needs no future act or validation to be complete. Teaching and healing are revealed to be both rhythmic and melodic, as we become whirling ecstatics spreading to a saddened culture our primal engagement and bliss. Even our necessary activism, and our most assertive resistance, are part of this dance. And there is no joy like that of helping other people, other species, other manifestations of Nature to be authentically realized, to bloom free and evolve unfettered. No greater satisfaction than helping them shine! It's here and now we choose to fly or fall...to ignore or heed the hero's call.

There may never be a period of total peace on Earth, and the truth is, we're strengthened and purified by a degree of challenge and travail. But there can and must be a return to balance that supports the flowering and blessing of the Whole. The necessary cure will involve a complete remaking or our sense of self, community, purpose, and place. It will require new forms of Earth-centered teaching, and teachers who are both visionary and grounded. A future founded in gratitude, and hope that will last. And a return to the sensibilities, sensitivities, and values of our sacramental tribal past. We can halt much of the destruction by exposing the facts, and through our most focused, unselfish acts. Even the earthquakes and droughts can be tempered, if not tamed, through the depth of our gratitude, the sincerity of our rituals, and the strength of prayers.

In bringing down a deer for food, our primitive ancestors of every race gave thanks. Indigenous Americans spread cornmeal before the animal's stilled mouth. An ocean away, early Indo-Europeans burned smudge sticks while describing their hungry children to their downed quarry, and promised to praise the creature's stamina and beauty in songs shared with the entire tribe. It's time that we, too, spread sacred yellow corn or hallowed tears at the foot of our many gifts. Time that we compose new songs to the source of our sentience and sustenance, bliss and delight. And that we sacrifice all delusion and hesitation on the miraculous altar of life.

If the extinction of humans ever happens, it will be because we neglected to respond as her "feelers" and healers, failed to fulfill our Gaian and evolutionary role. And if we survive the Earth changes and our own species' most magnificent mistakes, it will be because we have learned to apply the attendant lessons in ways that benefit not only us but the Earth. It's then that we'll truly flourish, body and soul...serving as her lovers and protectors, ritualists and restorationists, sensors and celebrants once again.

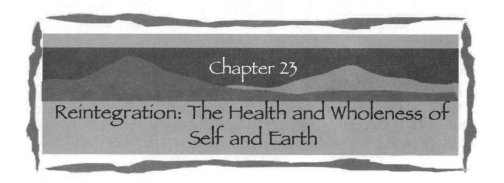

Chapter 23

Reintegration: The Health and Wholeness of Self and Earth

What lasts:
A strong will, like a muscle, like a rock.
The skeleton drinks from dirt. The lover
speaks from hardened bone
which lasts,
while faces, leaves, years do not.

—Barbara Mor

The Earth has repeatedly lost species to extinction, birdsongs never to be heard again. And like the land, I, too, have lost parts of myself—only to regain them through practice, prayer, personal insistence, and the passage of time. Things such as the willingness to laugh, and the ability to cry. The honest depths of agony, and far extremes of joy. My inner animal, and the reason for being. The inclination to play, and the patience to stay. It's a good thing, because the longer I'm here, the better able I am to hear the will and whisperings of the Earth...and the more myself I become.

Indeed, what is to be healthy, but to be whole: a balanced unity of gifts and needs, heart and mind, vision and action. Gaia teaches that good health isn't the absence of trauma or pain, but rather the most complete embodiment of our authentic selves. The depth of sensation, emotion, and experience. The fullness of expression and response. The fulfillment of our passions and our purpose, our destiny and our dreams. It's *how* we live, not *how long*. "Wellness" means living *well*: consciously and compassionately, artfully and purposefully.

It isn't disease that makes us unwhole, for pain makes us more aware of our bodies and feelings, and the way both our lifestyles and our immediate environments affect us. Suffering tempers our skills, tests our resolve, and strengthens our will. Debility teaches us humility, and infirmity counsels patience. The loss of one sensory organ leads to a honing of the others. At its worst, a deadly virus does nothing but return us to the Earth we arose from, extend from, and belong to. We are made unwhole not by death, but the failure to fully live. By that which dilutes our focus, weakens our intention, or dishonors our spirit. That which makes us doubt our instinct and intuition, significance or value. We are made unwhole by the suppression of our feelings, and the repression of our needs. By the subjugation of our animal beings. We have to give up certain aspects and components of ourselves, in order to fit into society's mold. It is the loss or neglect of these parts that contributes to our greatest dis-ease: our imagined separation from the rest of the living world. And with their re-membering and reclamation, we take the first of many steps towards the necessary cure.

Likewise, the Earth isn't made any less—or any less healthy—by the erosion of mountain rock into fertile valley soil, or the death of a cottontail in the jaws of a fox. Or even the shredding of forests by an erupting volcano, which grow back relatively quickly. Even the natural extinction of species is only a recycling of the parts into the Whole, each pruning results in a new burst of growth, an opportunity for new color and form. To the degree that it is sickened, it is not because of the annihilation of individual life-forms, but because of the overall reduction of biological, cultural, and topographical diversity. The extincting of species for no reasons other than obliviousness and greed. The appropriation of habitat, so there's little place left for the wildlife to spring back. The monocultures of agribusiness. And the genetic manipulation of life. And it's not just the killing off of native songbirds, but the hundreds of indigenous languages being lost to neglect. The defacing of the planet with asphalt, and the defaming with plastics. By our failing to notice Gaia's every miracle and gift, every hint of wind, the opening of a sidewalk blossom, the dance of a floating leaf. And by our forgetting to give thanks. We make the world sick with our neglect of self and planet, the dishonoring of Spirit, and the conceptual and physical dismembering of that which was one.

We say the "integrity" of a structure is compromised, and perhaps made unsafe, if any portion is degraded or removed. It is the same with a person or an ecosystem. The health of people or places increases with the diversity and magnitude of their expression. Thus any reduction in diversity impinges on the integrity of the Whole—and the role of the social and ecoactivist becomes one not only of resistance but restoration and reimmersion.

Our future personal, social, and ecological health may hinge on our personal integrity, and the surviving integrity of the natural world that we love. Like the extirpated Mexican gray wolf or the defamed spotted owl, we seek only to be and belong. For us, to be reintegrated is to be accepted back within the identity of the Gaian Whole, to exist and act in harmony with tribal human community and the community of Nature. Belonging is more than feeling settled, welcome, or even committed. It's the state of being at one with the needs, expression, and Spirit of the living, breathing Earth.

By learning to wholly serve, we intentionally rejoin the Whole. And it is through this bringing back together of disparate and damaged parts—of self and of Earth—that we never have to feel apart again.

Chapter 24

Harmony and Peace: A Gaian Perspective

Everything that happens is at once natural and inconceivable.
—E.M. Cioran

As I write this, the country is on the brink of yet another war waged against regimes and entities that in whatever ways have challenged our country's political and financial hegemony. And simultaneously, we continue to wage war on the Earth. You will recall that Europeans "discovered" in America a continent already inhabited by millions of indigenous peoples and billions of nonhuman species. They proceeded to "pacify" the native populations in deadly earnest, "capture" the mountain peaks, "tame" the rivers, and "conquer" the "virgin" wilderness. The analogy of an environmental war zone is all too real when viewed from the center of a devastated Oregon clear-cut, listening to the blast of high explosives at yet another dam site, or witnessing the Forest Service's bombardment of Vietnam-vintage napalm on eastern Texas forests to "save" them from insects. Even our pastoral road system is a veritable tomb to the community of life it encrusts.

As an empathic, I can't help but recoil from violence committed against anyone or anything, and I go out of my way to seek accord or accommodation...but I must confess, I am not a pacifist. I would surely and violently resist an attack on my life, the lives of my loved ones, or perhaps even the natural systems we and evolution depend upon. While I can sense and understand the internal anguish and suffering of my attackers, I invariably value my life more than I do theirs. Nor is my opposition to the latest flexing of military might based on any idealization of what we commonly call "peace." The concept of peace is too often used by the powers that be to disguise placation or control, conformity or stasis, tranquility or acceptance.

In many ways, this peace is a false ideal, which is why we find it so easily enlisted and promoted by warring states. Peace becomes their excuse, the resolution for which all wars are ostensibly fought. Armies "fight for peace." And peace is the way some describe those times of pacification between conflicts, when control and aggression are internalized by the population, when bribery and coercion stand in for raw force...and therefore, when power over the individual is complete. Like it or not, peace has been co-opted by the very interest groups who make political and financial gains off the suffering and subjugation of others.

My dictionary defines *peace* as "free of conflict or disturbance." But those of us involved in New Nature Spirituality know that there is no such peace anywhere in the natural world. The ocean named "Pacific," which means to pacify, is anything but tranquil. What appears as peaceful is the occasionally calm surface, concealing mighty currents underneath. Nature's diverse expressions are the result of determined individuation. Life's many shapes are formed by the tension between opposed forces. Life exists by feeding on life, the aggressive act of predation. Scientists have demonstrated what primitive people knew long ago: even plants experience pain. Vegetarianism seems peaceful largely because we fail to hear their screams.

In the Gaian world, red-tailed hawks feast on scrambling cottontails, buck deer crash into one another during rut, trout chase other fish well away from their spawning grounds, and squirrels defend their nests with vicious bites and a furious stamping of paws. Aggression provides a service for the natural world, earning each species the food it eats, the certain passing down of the strongest genetic traits, the survival of their young, the inviolability of their niche, and the integrity of their life's unmanipulated dance.

Other than hunting for sustenance, aggression in the animal world seldom results in death. Wolf packs do not form alliances to drive their prey to extinction. Even among tribal peoples, alliances were limited to shared bioregions, and the greatest honor in a conflict was to shame the other warrior by touching him without killing him: "counting coup." Modern warfare, on the other hand, is depersonalized aggression—institutionalized violence on a massive scale.

The development of awesome new technological weaponry parallels the dehumanization of aggression and the devaluing of life. We have thermonuclear warheads with the power to destroy every living thing on the planet many times over, poised to strike people we will never know well enough to find a reason to hurt. Civilization has debased our animus, robbed us of our true nature. It has led us to fear without understanding, consume without hunger, lust without loving, and kill without passion.

Indeed, modern war is founded on and fed by alienation and abstraction, not anger. Soldiers are taught to feel no emotions as they "neutralize" their targets. Mass genocide is a product of our depersonalization more than our wrath. And the anger of its victims and witnesses can fuel compassionate but forceful resistance to the ponderous machinery of destruction. Getting mad is a valid and perhaps crucial response to the cutting of the last ancient redwoods, the obliteration of the last wild wolf, or missile attacks on any people or land. Imprisoned for beating on live warheads with carpenter's hammers, the Plowshares Eight functioned not just as consciousness-raisers, but as counterbalances to the state of repression. The hundreds of conscientious protesters arrested each year for trespassing at the Nevada nuclear test site are honorable antidotes. Surely in the looming shadow of Armageddon, it is feeling nothing and doing nothing that is most wrong of all.

The Hopi have a word for the current separative, technological age: *Koyanasquaatsi*, meaning "world out of balance." War will end not when we "establish peace," but when we return to life-in-balance, to an equilibrium not only between each other but between human kind and all other elements of Nature as well. In dance it is called choreography. In music we refer to this balancing and cooperating of differing tones as *harmony*, searching out sympathetic pitch and vibration. Harmony between people would mean humanity's diverse voices somehow learning to perform together for the greater good. And unlike what we may hear touted as "inner peace," inner harmony is not so much an end to contest or ambivalence as the successful orchestration of our own contending voices, of our competing priorities, and sometimes contradictory needs.

Separative acculturation removes us from the natural composition. As a society we are increasingly segregated from the tonal symmetry, the congruity of contiguous elements in perfect balance with one another. The aim of New Nature Spirituality is not only to find peace—those moments of quiet between notes—but also to guarantee human reapportionment within life's "movement." It can be our minstrelsy, a contribution to balance within relationship, and a melodious resistance. As we transition from the scorekeeping of war to the musical score, we fulfill our rhythmic purpose, reintegrate in the greater "arrangement" of indivisible Nature.

In times of unparalleled destruction, the last thing we need is more simple acceptance, misspent tolerance, or pacification. The peace we believe in is proactive not passive, dynamic not static. It is a condition of active cooperation between different parts of the self or between different people, groups, or nations.

We are each called to reawaken and redouble our efforts, to reorchestrate the madness our civilization has wrought. In this heroic service, our maestro's baton doubles as a magic wand...insistently invoking a return to the balance of a dynamic, heartful, and harmonic Whole.

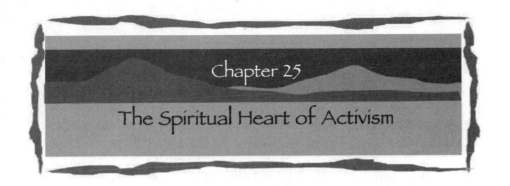

Chapter 25

The Spiritual Heart of Activism

A man who possesses a veneration of life will not simply say his prayers. He will throw himself into the battle to preserve life, if for no other reason that he himself is an extension of life around him.

—Albert Schweitzer

One who performs acts of heroism puts himself in contact with the supernatural. The reward of heroism is not personal glory nor riches. The reward is dreams.

—Gary Snyder

The most powerful social and environmental activism is inspired, fed, and sustained by spiritual sensibility and magical practice. And the most powerful spirituality or practice is inevitably rooted in place: in the human and more-than-human history of the land where the practices are based, and in the inspirited Earth itself.

Periodically for 15 years, I suffered having to leave the canyon where I belong, but it was for all the right reasons. I traveled the length and breadth of this country giving talks and performing concerts that resulted not only in the formation of new activist groups, the raising of support and funds for the various regional campaigns, and the inspiration of audiences...but often in their participation in direct actions following the shows. My cohorts and I enlisted art and ritual in the service of the Okenagan Mountains, which are jeopardized by cyanide leach mining, grizzly bear habitat protection, and the restoration of riparian zones. The gatherings usually concluded with group hugs, in powerful circles of teary eyed seekers, in howls and hopes, and spiral dances that burst out of the school halls and out onto the grass and into the rain. When pressed to describe the Deep Ecology Medicine Shows, one student said, "It was like a ceremony affirming life, a ritual awakening my power to do something about the many problems we face."

It may be the same for conservative suit-wearing environmental professionals as those hardcore anarchist protesters that dismiss all ritual as meaningless "woo-woo." While they may not be aware of the fact, most, if not all, ecological activists are informed and inspired by an emotional, cellular, energetic connection to the imperiled Earth that is nothing less than spiritual. And it has always been so. Creator of a new land ethic, Aldo Leopold described his experience killing a she-wolf, "watching the green fire in her eyes die," as a spiritual epiphany. John Muir, grandfather of the American conservation movement, was a wild-eyed Irishman given to dramatic exclamations and acts. Books show grained black-and-white images of an aging man at rest at his desk, posing uncomfortably in a photographer's studio, or standing placidly on a Yellowstone overlook with an imperturbable president, Theodore Roosevelt. But I picture him as he was when he was most moved, hootin' and hollerin' on a makeshift whitewater raft, in rapt intercourse with a line of forest ants, or struck breathless by an awesome new vista. Perched at the spindly top of a giant conifer tree in the middle of a raging storm, swept by the wind into a giant arc, his eyes lit up by flashes of lightning—now there's an image of a man whose explorations of the natural world were nothing less than revelatory. He was, in every way, enraptured. In the ways of plants and beasts, he found deep communion, and this revelation included a calling to protect and preserve that which he had grown to love.

There's a powerful story in the way the village women of the Southern Himalayas banded together to stop deforestation uphill of their villages. They acted not only to reduce the instances of dangerous mudslides, but to honor and protect the divas, or spirits, of the trees themselves. Because of their risky tactic of throwing their arms around pines about to be cut, their cultural and environmental movement is called "Chipko," a Sanskrit word meaning literally "to embrace." Australian rainforest activist John Seed talks about nurturing a spiritual connection between himself and the trees, to the degree that when the chainsaw bites into their flesh, he feels it ripping into his own side as well. Redwood heroine Julia Butterfly Hill writes that it was her spiritual connection to the tree she called "Luna," that allowed her to stay up in it so many months while besieged with police loudspeakers, loggers' saws, and winter storms assaulting her tiny aerial platform.

The construction of giant telescopes atop Arizona's "sky island" Mt. Graham has been vigorously opposed by both environmental groups and native traditionalists. Resistance and ritual go hand in hand in the "sacred runs" regularly held by the Apache. In July of 1993, I participated in one of many protests involving Earth First! and the Mt. Graham Coalition. We ignored the sheriff's orders not to proceed, and walked the rest of the way up the mountain to the chain-link fences surrounding the telescopes. Sweating from the heat of the ascent, and deeply moved by the destruction we saw, everyone dropped to the dusty ground in a spontaneous circle of grief and prayer. Through our tears we spoke as witnesses, shared our pain, begged forgiveness for being part of a culture that disregards the relevance of wildness, of places of power, and of the beliefs and traditions of the resident indigenous people. One man spoke for the endangered Mt. Graham red squirrel, and a woman heavy with child bemoaned giving birth in an age when nothing—not even the Earth we depend upon—is held sacred anymore. Together we asked for guidance from the spirits of the mountain, the strength to continue the struggle of love and life no matter what the obstacles or results.

It's difficult to maintain your energy and mood in the face of too many reversals, and this is especially true of the committed activist. A case in point occurred during a protest of clear-cuts in the then pristine Kalmiopsis Wilderness of southeastern Oregon in 1988. Following an unexpected sweep by the Josephine County Sheriff's Department, 24 of us found ourselves under arrest and locked inside a paddy wagon with barred windows. Rather than transport us to jail right away, we were left in the sweltering metal van for hours while the logging company downed the very grove we were hoping to save, right before our eyes. We comforted and encouraged ourselves by singing various songs by Si Kahn and Walkin' Jim Stoltz, and by reaching out together to a creative force that includes us, but is so much bigger than any immediate person, group, or trauma.

When an activist is arrested, it is often a deliberate choice. Especially when doing blockades or other civil disobedience actions, the protester volunteers to be arrested, humiliated, fingerprinted, jailed, and fined...in order to confront the perpetrators of destruction, attract media, instruct the masses, and draw attention to the plight of a people, species, or place. Putting their bodies on the line is making their love real and manifest, a way of "walking the talk," turning rhetoric into risk and response. They risk losing their jobs when the boss hears. Risk being beaten if the police get out of control. It is their rite of passage into responsible adulthood, their way of giving something back. It is their glad sacrifice.

The word "sacrificial" derives from the same root as the word "sacred." When we sacrifice schedules and habits, predisposition and profit, and ultimately our lives on the altar of our love...we do so as part of a sacred calling. Not out of atonement of our own or others' sins, but to give a little of ourselves back to the powers and place that gave us birth. The young man on a tripod in front of the Biotech industry gates is a teen Odin hanging from the tree of knowledge. The group of Bikini Islanders, elderly Japanese, and Utah mothers stepping over the line at the Nevada nuclear test site, share more than hot, brittle ground with the distant Indian fakir sitting in lotus on his hard rock perch. A woman, her neck fastened to a Pacific Lumber Company gate with a Kryptonite bicycle lock, a can of mace being shoved in her face, draws strength picturing a praying Sioux sun-dancer, with buffalo skulls hung from bleeding skewers in his chest.

When deciding what actions are needed in defense of the Earth, we are called to go directly to the source. By silencing the verbose mind and opening to the meaning-filled signals from the rest of the living planet, we create the condition of respect necessary for rapport. It is our natural, if often suppressed ability, to communicate with the other agents of the Earthen Whole, to serve as a conduit for their expression, and to send our own response back to the Whole, informing it as it informs us. And acting in ways that heal self, community, and planet—as instruments of the Whole and holy All.

Whatever one calls it, there's an undeniable force that courses through this planet, a vibrational unity, an underlying if mysterious pattern—an entity of inclusion that animates, inspires, enlightens, and fuels the evolution of the spiritual as well as bodily forms of its participant beings. Even the most mental, and the most clueless of us can get it. We know it as children, but then at some point we agree to join the collective denial. I grew up in major cities with little or no healthy spirituality from which to refer or to learn. I was affected not by engaged people and examples of activism, so much as by distracted masses and creeping complacency. And like most in the American culture, I was surrounded by attitudes of apathy and atheism, technological monuments to scientific query. Yet nothing I read or witnessed diminished the reality of the mysterious and the miraculous. I still recognized a numinous presence in all things, and found it first and foremost in what I could find of the natural world: in starling squatters taking over hollow street signs, ivy sucking the facades off of pretentious government buildings, and the always untamable weather. I felt it just beneath the pavement, pregnant with swelling seed and palpable purpose: a wildness of spirit, and the Spirit of the Earth.

We are both blessed and cursed with the unique ability to self-reflect, and thus to imagine ourselves as separate from the rest of the sacred, ecological Whole. Those accepting of the living Earth have always moved close to the ground in order to better hear the Shamans of Tuva throat-singing on the dirt floors, Native Americans vision-questing in dug-out pits, and the early Irish watching for signs and omens inside the "Tigh'n alluis," the Celtic sweat lodge. The most valid understanding of the workings of this planet are more likely to result from personal intimacy with the flesh of its being than from clever conclusion. Our role within this Whole is clarified not by taking charge, but by adjusting ourselves, our plans, and our modes of perception in ways that bring us closer in tune with the extant will of the holy, wholesome, planet organism.

We seek the guidance of Mother Earth, of Gaia, through our relationship with a particular, specific place—a place we've come to know well and deeply appreciate. For me it is a certain bend in the St. Francis River, that even now I ache to return to. For others it may be a treasured camping spot, a prominent peak just outside of town, or an enchanted section of their own backyard. In this way we contact the entire universe through the eternity of a single touch. It is the way of our hunter-gatherer foremothers and forefathers, the way of intense and intentional Nature, the way of Spirit incarnate.

Our ancient ancestors believed and acted as if the world would end if they ever failed to properly carry out their rituals on time. And in essence it was true, for the ceremonies grounded the people in right relationship with the Earth, without which the people could not survive. A people divorced from the ways of Nature must eventually perish as a result of this estrangement, and then for them, at least, the world would have indeed come to an end. It is no different for us now. Without a reciprocal, ritual relationship with the natural world, without those feats of ceremony and sentience that reunite us with the Earthen body, we are fated to endlessly repeat our most debilitating mistakes. All that stands between a healthy planet and nuclear or biological meltdown is us ourselves, and the ways we choose to perceive, relate to, and resacrament the living world of which we are a part.

All ritual raises power, but none more so than the rituals that are growing out of the contemporary context, the needs of the people and the place—right now, right here. The Great Spirit didn't just reveal itself to our progenitors and then withdraw, leaving only commandments behind for us descendants. No! Whatever we choose to call the inspirited All, the instructions are nonetheless still there to be read in the text of living creation. Revelation remains readily available to the seeker, directly, with no institutional agents or professional intermediaries to confuse, dilute, or derange.

Of course, it's ideal when our rituals and our activism also affirm the common values, desires, and needs of whatever community we are a part of. Together the people of the community can develop rites and ceremonies that mirror and focus our shared connection to the customs of culture, the relations of family, and the fiestas, celebrations, and demonstrations of grief that characterize them. These ways of being and acting are not New Age, but "first nature": of our nature, and of the natural world.

New Nature Spirituality is embodied in the child saddened by the sight of a butterfly bounced off a windshield onto the shoulder of some numbered road...and in an old woman finding reason to go on living in the slow unfolding of a window-box flower. It is voiced in the sermon-scream of falcons feeding on pigeons in downtown New York City, in the spontaneous living prayers of outlaw dandelions erupting in the cracks of every aging sidewalk, in a liturgy recorded in the spiraling reggae of the DNA helix and the twisting conga line of ants ascending a gnarled cottonwood. Its only commandments are "written in stone" in the many "rocks of ages": a testament in limestone, granite, and quartz; a demonstration of and demand for authenticity and substance; and the weight and substance of one's commitment to place. Its message is carried on the lift of robins' songs, and delivered on the backs and in the hearts of every activist devoted to this Earth's protection.

Spirituality is not just the inspiration and reward. It's part of the "great work," the most crucial mode of awakeness, perception, and connection—the means to the fulfillment of our most meaningful purpose. It is both the literal and liturgical ground for a new start. It is activism's true heart.

Chapter 26

Gaia River

Don't let them tame you!

—Isadora Duncan

From the time I was little, I knew I had to live close to the water. Not the majestic ocean, mind you—too salty to drink, too turgid to see into the depths for what might eat the swimming, wondering boy. Nor would the most beautiful or serene lake do, its stillness an indictment of my youthful restless nature. I knew somehow that it would have to be a river next to which I'd make my lifetime home. Its song would be the sound of "a different drummer" that I marched to, rocked-out to, danced the samba to. It would be the soundtrack of my life, its murmurings inundating my dreams. Its drone would be my comforting lullaby, even as its splashes and gurgles kept a part of me forever awake.

Because of the way it snakes back and forth between the walls of the canyon, a visitor has to wade the same river seven times to get here. Think: Steve Young's "Seven Bridges Road." The seven voyages of Sinbad. The seven sacred gates leading to paradise. And seven potentially Jeep-swallowing crossings. Lucky seven, indeed. At its highest our river functions as a moat, effectively keeping the 21st century out. (I like to picture it stocked with alligators, specially bred to feed on real-estate agents, and yet tame enough for the local kids to ride.) Even when it's so low a sober man could jump over, it still has the effect of looking like your new truck might get stuck. Like a sleeping guard dog, its appearance alone is usually enough to guarantee our privacy, and ensure this sanctuary's continuing wildness.

Introducing the Rio Frisco, the St. Francis, patron river of the Gila's animals. Needless to say, becoming sainted is no simple matter. It requires being originally blessed, suffering misunderstanding and repression, being tragically martyred, and then having its unique goodness missed. It had to be reborn, and brought back to life first *in the mind*.

And so it was. For eons the Frisco was the lifeblood of the four-legged and green-growing beings, and it was long the spiritual fountain of the native pit-house dwellers that anthropologists call the Mogollon. Then came the suffering and plague, with more than a century of overgrazing by immigrant Texas cattle. Elder cottonwoods lost to the occasional flood were no longer being replaced, as the sprouts of alamo and willow alike were gobbled up by the voracious cows. The river no longer channelized, but wandered from one side of the canyon to the other, as if trying to avoid its tormentors. In time, this was followed by the idea of a river reborn, and then the opportunity and determination to act on it. We were literally the first protectors in a thousand years, fencing off parts of the river, replanting and restoring its banks until at least one section of the canyon was a riparian forest again. The St. Francis, the "sweet medicine" river, healed...and now healing those who come open to her gifts.

We're quick to tell folks we live on a river. No one really lives "on" a river, of course, unless they're on a houseboat on the constipated Colorado River, or a converted shrimper anchored in Roy Orbison's blue bayou. More specifically, we live in intimate *proximity* to a river, *akin* to a river—far enough to keep the foundation of the cabin dry, close enough that our lives become dependent on and sculpted by its flux and flow. In its waters we witness the rise and fall of dream and fortune, and the passage of our lives. We discover ourselves in its reflection, our moods ranging from tickle and trickle to murky depression, from shallow to deep, alert or asleep. Like the river, we can be shrunken and tentative, hiding and sliding between meager bastions of rock, our temperatures determined by the heat and cold of that which surrounds us, lacking enough elemental confidence to float a fish. Or we can be full of ourselves, spilling out over our edges, exceeding the capacity of our containers, expanding beyond our imagined limitations as we seek to penetrate and inundate the universe.

The Frisco is a wild river, make no mistake. Wild as the geese that never land, and those watchful heron that do. Wild as the winds that hump the ever blushing cliffs, as the thorny rose or the undisciplined twists of wild grape vine. Not "wild" as in "dangerous and unpredictable," but as in "willful" and "willed": internally directed and unapologetically purposeful. Untamed, but not without compassion or reason. Water with a message. Water with a mission.

Water born of the mountains.

Rivers and mountains—even the words seem as if they are meant to be together, curled up back to belly on the lap of the tongue. Like a couple who have been married for a long, long time, it gets hard to talk about one and not the other. "Where would she be without him?" someone might ask. "He's not happy unless she is," you must agree. They start each day with a wet kiss, finish each others' sentences, and never sleep alone. If one were to die, the other would surely perish soon after. Not just of need, but of a terrible loneliness.

The music that had varied from seductive tinkle to fulsome roar becomes a whisper where the mountains are no more. Once a river enters a valley, it widens and seems to lose its intensity, as if away from its alpine lover it no longer has any reason to display its rage, nor to impress or to play. A force that once cut through rock, now gently soaks into its grassy sides. It seems to lose some of its interest, if not its way.

We don't have a lot of water in the Southwest, and that makes it all the more precious. The less there is of it, the bigger it grows in our imaginations. When you've got cottonmouth and an empty canteen, every rain-catch in the sandstone high country looks puddle-lickin' good. Our few lakes look like giant oceans of drinkable water, a gift from or for the gods. Anytime a stream drops over a 4-foot rock, it's a waterfall. Get your clothes off and get under it, if you don't believe me. A river is any moving body of liquid big enough to lay down in, or any dry-bed that it's not safe to build a house near. We call New Mexico's largest river the "Rio Grande," meaning grand—nobly huge—even though it's shallow enough that a person making his way across never gets more than his knees wet, and it would take hundreds of such rios to fill the bed of the Missouri or Mississippi Rivers. Most of our rivers are of a size they call creeks, or "cricks" in other parts of the country, other than during those Spring runoffs or the rare Fall cloudburst when they've been known to give week-long workshops in humility. Just ask the smug tourist who drives up the edge of one our cherished flows, a disapproving scowl on his twisted little face.

"Why, that's no river. Back where I come from, we'd call this a..." he might start, before his words, along with his shiny little car, are washed downstream in front of a muddy wall of water barreling for Arizona. It was 1983 when our own dear Frisco rose from calf deep to 30 feet deep, scouring the canyon walls and rolling giant boulders that rumbled like the thunderous bowling lanes of Rip Van Winkle's cloud-wrapped Valhalla. The highlights included waving off the National Guard helicopter that came to check on us, and using an antique Winchester to take potshots at the taillights of poor old Pete Daniel's mobile home as it bobbed on by. No one watching its turgid swells in flood stage could call it a creek, a stream, or anything but a river. One *hell* of a river.

Sadly, we know that even the largest watercourses around here never make it to the ocean. From the beginning there is competition for the resource, water lawyers screwing the locals for their water rights, and selling them out of state at enormous profit. What's left is coveted by nesting water-fowl and feeding kingfishers, the remaining native willows and giant cotton-woods, and the invasive Asian tamarisk with its greedy roots and gorgeous purple plumes. The rivers are diverted by a thousand acequias into fields of cotton and chili, and sucked dry by desert sunshine. They get shallower and shallower after they leave New Mexico, until there's nothing left. The subter-ranean aquifers that would normally replenish them are drained for the blue-grass sprinklers and built-in swimming pools of El Paso and Tucson. They fill the water coolers of underpaid Juarez workers making designer tennies for the discount chains up North. Follow any one downstream and you will even-tually notice the smell of baking algae and dead fish, their hollow eyes look-ing incredulously for the world, and the water, that once sustained them. These are the places where hope itself seems to vanish in the sand.

Downhill is far too easy, of course, for certain hard-headed hikers and spiritual seekers. We head upstream to the source instead, and not just to-wards the headwaters, but the pinnacles of balance, the very source of peace. Toward the high peaks of the contemplative hermit, the mountain man, the wild woman "La Loba," and the self-sacrificing Penitente seeking his own per-sonal cross of trial and redemption. Towards the abode of the ancient tribes-man on a vision quest to find meaning and purpose, authentic self, and the Great Spirit, the great mystery. And of the mountain goat, the watchful elk, the herb-gathering bear. It is here that the rain first settles into channels, coupling with other rivulets, chasing and playing in moves that appear like falling, but may be the result of desire. Each intercourse results in something bigger, something more than the sum of its parts.

To truly enter the kingdom of the river, we have to shed all our precon-ceptions, unhitch our insistent thoughts, strip down to skin, and really take the river in. Hence the spiritual dimension. The river soothes our souls, and fuels our hungers. It cleanses and unites. It dies for our sins, rolls away the rock, and lives again.

A river can seem cruel at times, when it carves away at the land, or is the cause of a careless child losing its life. Over the centuries, entire towns have been leveled by rivers' rushing waters. But we must wonder if what appears to be a senseless tragedy may really be a vital lesson, or part of a greater plan. How can we who see only a single bend, know the intentions of an entire watershed? Yea, the river doth work in mysterious ways. It giveth water, food, and soil, and then it taketh away.

Who shall ever know the river, shall know themselves. Ask and ye shall drink. By approaching it consciously, we become participants in a sort of ri-parian Chautauqua, a riverine revival. We join with the crowds of buzzing bees and spinning dragonflies, attendant trees and rapt grass. We babble in the tongues of terns and frogs. We kneel down in the front rows, and are some of the first to come forward when the moment arrives to be anointed by its waters, to be made whole by its touch. We each come to be washed. No one comes to the river clean.

Our job as riverside residents is to learn to honor not only its incarnation and blessings, but also its spirit and needs—and to serve its will. We do so by setting aside days of rest and reflection, wordless communion, and songs of praise. By planting seeds and taking comfort under the bushes that grow. We lay willow boughs at its feet, that they might propagate and prosper. We watch that no one poisons it with pollutants or other indignities, and do whatever we can to repair the damage that's been done before. To give our hearts and hours over to the care of damaged and dying waters.

Of course, the last wild and natural places aren't so much dying, as being killed. And in the metaphor of rivers we seek not only consolation, but retribution, reclamation, and resolution, as ecotroubadour Dana Lyons sings in "Drop of Water," a piece he wrote as we watched the Frisco rise:

"Watch the current become a stream, busting through the seams," the song begins.

"Cracking through the concrete, bending down the steel, in a raging that is real, a tearing torrent you can feel."

I think it was a show in Olympia, Washington, where the audience spontaneously linked up like mischievous molecules of water, arm in arm, forming their own insistent river. Ecotroubadour Dana Lyons sang the heart of the river while I drummed its rising waters, drummed hurt and anger, drummed thunder and love.

"And now the river, and now the river is freeeeee..."

Faster and faster they circled, kicking the cheap metal chairs out of the way. It was the Kaliyuga unleashed, the opportunity for both cleansing and redemption. It was the world snake uncoiling, spiraling out of control, and then out into the pouring rain. We could see them weaving and throbbing in Dionysian delight, much to the amazement of the sorority sisters staring out of their upper story windows in disbelief.

"And in my heart, the chains falling apart."

For what seemed like an eternity, we were left playing to an empty room, discarded shoes and fallen chairs marking the high-water tide of a primal human flood. Then they spilled back in, still linked, still seeking resolution, seeking the moment of feeling complete—a returning to the welcoming sea.

"And for once in my life I know I'm not alone, for the mountains make our bones."

The energy was still going strong the following day, as half the audience made it to a nearby protest site, their hearts emboldened against the dragon of avarice and apathy. This is what we look for in a social or environmental revolution. One voice growing into many. The hundredth monkey getting up to dance, provoking and inspiring the world to dance with her. The building up of momentum, of a movement of peace and justice and unblighted wilderness that no damn dam could ever stop.

The San Francisco River winds through the high country, gathering stories as it goes—a natural and human history inextricably woven together through this common need, common home. It passes near the site of Aldo Leopold's "Greenfire" story, the alpine meadow where his killing of a wolf led to the writing of a compelling new land ethic. It's here that the first wolves to roam the Southwest in 25 years were released by the U.S. Fish and Wildlife Service as part of its reintroduction program. These are the soft banks where Victorio and Geronimo once rested, after doing their part to slow down mining and development in the sacred Gila River. It carries me not only into a colorful past and uncertain future, but also deeper into the canyons of the here and now.

Truth is, there's nowhere else for me, no longer anywhere else I can be. I've already spent far too much time traveling and giving talks about what it means to be a caretaker of home, while the place I loved was neglected and alone.

Sense of place is a product of intimacy as much as grace. If we claim to love all rivers equally, we spread our time among many, and may get to know none well. Likewise, none may claim us as their own. By focusing on only a few, we're brought deeper into the labyrinth of their whorls, welcomed as residents of their swirling worlds. Pledge to a single waterway and we become privy to its every secret, earn its unconditional trust. We occupy a common vessel, a common desire and form.

There's a reason they call it a river "bed," this place for the demonstration of passion. It is where water lies down with sand and stone, and where we lie down with water. It is not still, but laps upon us, leaving nothing private, no place unhandled. Bubbles titillate, gravel shifts provocatively beneath us, a slippery fish slides under our legs. We are both held and massaged. We feel the weighty, undulating presence of our paramour between our arms, and we find ourselves hugging the river in return.

From the Amazon to the Tiger, the frigid Yellowstone to the temperate Frisco, river folk hold to some pretty similar ideas. Foremost is that there is something like water, continuous and contiguous, of which we're a lasting part. Here perhaps is the real meaning of the expression "going with the flow."

Not directionless, but moving in the same direction as Nature and evolution, in the direction of evolving Spirit. We believe that like the river, we are forever changing. Yet somehow we stay—something of us will always remain. That we, too, are dissolved by the sun and then return like the rain.

A friend used to kid me that in Navajo, *sacred* means "don't mess with it." There's more to it than that, of course. As any feral or aboriginal river-lover will tell you, that which is sacred desires and deserves our tending. Not only protecting, but nourishing and celebrating. The lesson may be that all things natural have an intrinsic sacred value, but through ritual, attention, and intent, we make them even more so: Investing the rocks with centuries of prayer. Impregnating the soil with our promises. Swelling the river with generations of practiced magic and directed love. It's often a part of the belief systems of those peoples living closest to the land...that the river knows when we're singing to it, and knows when we've stopped. And that it holds in its bowels the memories of all life's songs.

Chapter 27

Living Art: The Ritual of Expression

Culture comes up out of the earth, vibrating through the body, as each individual affirms life and expresses her or his unique creativity. It is kept alive by consciously honoring the sacredness of the four Great Mysteries: food, sex, birth, and death. The ceremonial arts are channels for people to express their relationship with these primal mysteries.

—Sedonia Cahill

We're connected to each other, to self, and to home through blood and bone, history and need, touch and love—and through the expression of our magical beings, the moving force of art.

Art and love are surely among humanity's most redeeming graces. And the most meaningful of that art reflects, exalts, and is informed by inspirited Nature. It's an acknowledgment and glorification of the inner essence of relationship and form, of that numinous essence that our creations can only allude to at best. It is the marriage of symbol and context, Earth and Spirit.

Art is vision made visible, Spirit made physical, fostered and nurtured by loving hands, drawn from a palette of mountain clay and Earthen pigment...of pain and joy, struggle and reward. It is the combination of this deep Earthen connection and intense intentionality that makes real art something more than decoration, raising it to the level of ritual and magic. The artist celebrates not only the lines and color of a particular landscape, but the character that breeds and defines its landed features, the spirits of place honored in deft strokes by one who loves the land in the hush of compost and gray of winter as much as the brilliant warmth of Spring greens. And it is just as true for our poetry, correspondence, and diary entries; for craft and song and dance dedicated to the illumination of the lasting inner power; the energetic fibers that connect us to the Whole. Dances to the hunted animals, chants to the rain gods, magical paintings on mats of bark and myths told and retold over the proverbial tribal fire—all are stories, and it is story that binds us to our beliefs, to the past and the future, and to the experience of place. They are the threads that weave us back into our contact with the land that defines and sustains us, crucial lessons handed down through the inheritance of crafts rather than the sequencing of genes.

Since the very beginnings of what it means to be "human," we have venerated and exalted the gods and goddesses, the inspirited land, and our true loves—and it is in this place of art and ritual where we know these things and ourselves as one. It was the pale villagers of Paleo-Europe who left us the sculpted body of the archetypal Earth Mother, their cave walls filled with the evocations of magic. Similarly, the ancient pueblo people of the Southwest left behind sherds of painted pottery that continue to evoke the Great Mystery—fired clay fragments of a life of reverence, picture-puzzle pieces still vibrating with the energy of years of honoring touch. They spoke their fealty for the land in rock art carved out of their collective and individual souls, lightning bolts and the seed-carrier Kokopelli painted on the sides of the caves. Here, too, are the forms of the artists' fingers and palms—their signatures, the marks of their selves—in graphic hands reaching out to their descendants across the chasm of time. They left enduring images of their priorities and loves, deities and dreams. They left their holiest expressions of wonder and communion, the evidence of a marriage with place consecrated in timeless art.

What is often missing in our contemporary, unlanded culture is not merely artistic form *in* life, but the art *of* life: the art of conscious, responsive, celebratory relationship. The assignment is not only to make the relationship work, but to make it beautiful as well! Not only meeting the needs of the other, but delighting them with our means for doing so. In our relationship to the land, the care we gift it includes our attentiveness, love, protection, and artful celebration of shared being. In our ecstatic coming together, there is the opportunity for a further dissolving of boundaries. Boundaries between us and the land. Between the creative force and what has been created, the artist and the art.

Too often in this society we relegate art to those visible forms seeming to exist beyond ourselves, to finished and salable products rather than recognizing it as an ongoing process in which we play an essential role. Say the word "art" and many will conjure images of mummified paintings hung in sterile museums, the tastier graphics adorning the expressway billboards or the better of the year's dramatic films. For some, art is whatever catches and pleases the eye so long as it was informed by the human hand, while for others it can only be found in the few of those creations that manage to stand out from the rest, enlisting, stirring, and releasing our reservoirs of pent-up emotion. Others find an artistic perfection one can barely approximate on paper or in clay in the creations of Nature or God, in the luster of the sunset and the grace of beating wings. And in the end, all our art, as all people and all life forms...is of the Earth. Grounded in a wild and creative Nature, empowered by Spirit.

What nearly all of us forget is the degree to which we can and should be participants in the artistry in which we're immersed. While we may consider ourselves "spectators," we inevitably contribute awareness, experience, and emotion to what is principally an exchange. Exchanges with someone's painting, with the architecture that surrounds us, or the heavy-breathing clouds above our heads. Indeed, we are all artists, with a chance to make our lives into art. We each leave an imprint on the world, and we can make it a true reflection of our authentic spirits. Every act, every motion or gesture of our hands can be the art that communicates who we are and who we strive to be. We are artists, sensually immersed and engaged in a world of art. The swaying pines, the outlawed dandelions, the look in a sweetheart's eye: art, significance, and meaning. The facade of a old Victorian building, a crusty cowboy strumming out a song for his wife of 30 years, the way a snowboarder banks and spins, even a single fully conscious breath: art. We are ever creator as well as audience, helping to make and remake the moment with our participation, our willingness to look and feel, and our insistence on being real.

Maybe that's how we tell what true art is, by what it is *not*: not phony, not pretentious, not faking it for laughs or begging for sympathy. It doesn't make excuses, plead for forgiveness, or demand obedience. It is a reflection of all that is, and at the same time it is unique and like no other poem or painting or tattoo in the world—and thus, it is not always comfortable. It can be a sharing of fears that somehow raises our hopes, as well as a display of unbearable beauty. Humor and sobriety, wildness and reflection, death and rebirth. It may seem to fit too tight or leave us too much room. Reveal disruptive truths or show too much skin. Its horrors recall our mortality, its luminescence drawing attention to our every untended and unfulfilled dream.

As disassociated as we may sometimes feel from the processes of art, there is a child still alive in us that still loves to draw, to handle a sharp pencil, to splash watercolors, or to inhale the aroma of the turpentine and linseed oil that thins and binds the pigments to canvas. Vision can be as immediate as touch—direct and with no need of explanation. Like priests and priestesses, we ceremonially ready the vacant sheets of tree-flesh, release our life force in a fountain of red paints, freed of all preconceptions about design as meaning proceeds to take over. One never really manufactures either adventure or art. We are confronted by it, consumed by it...and remade within it! It always has a purpose, one beyond the range of the artist's intentions, and it is willingly given away. Here today and gone tomorrow, like those golden cottonwood leaves. Like those Tibetan sand paintings intricately crafted in this ever-shifting medium, definitive colors sure to blow across one another, mixing and blending until fully melded into, fully indifferentiable from the landscape from which they came. But then it's not in the completion of some project that we become fulfilled. Rather, it is in the making of our art, in the living of our lives that we're made whole.

"The purpose of art is not to represent the outward appearance of things, but their inner significance," Aristotle proclaimed. This is true for those aesthetic forms evolved independent of human influence as much as for our "own" creations: for rivers and twisted cedar limbs as well as the sculpture forming beneath the attentive motion of our tools. Each glinting rock, each flex of river muscle is an inspiration to the heart, and food for soul. Art is what comes of the relationship between self and other when allowed to express itself. It is a complex and evolving structure for relating that we exist and act within. With or without the artist's brush, we reach out to make our mark, from the center of our experience of art, of life, of our mated land.

In the artist's vernacular, our attention to form is called "style." Once we've made art into a way of being, an activity, a *verb*, we see the ways in which it corresponds to the word "grace," which can mean a "seemingly effortless beauty or charm of movement," "an excellence bestowed by God," and "a prayer of thanksgiving." It is in this sense of motive beauty, beneficence, and gratitude that we impart grace to our acts, and are in turn graced by the inspired world we act upon and within.

Repetitive chores turn into art whenever they're executed with style, then they become ritual concurrent with our conscious acknowledgment of their meaning and importance. The same acts completed without our mindful attention and conscious intent are simply habits. We don't need to take time away from living to engage in ritual, so much as we need to ritualize our daily existence. Sitting up in bed each morning to face the first sun becomes a ritual as soon as we're conscious of it as an act of interpenetration and show of gratitude. The sharing of food moves from a quick refueling to a slow and artful unfolding, and then into ritual as each serving is consecrated, every bite undertaken as communion. Communion with the life-forms that feed us, with the sun and rain and soil that made the salad possible, with the spiritual and evolutionary power moving through both consumer and consumed.

The result is reconnection, as our art and practice weaves us back into the *material* of our experience. Together with the ritual efforts of others, we co-create the living fabric of culture, jointly paint on that fabric the story of our struggles, our miracles...*our beautiful, beautiful hope.*

Chapter 28

The Magic Drum: Rhythm and Nature

*A working religion might be one that binds together the many
rhythms that affect us by creating techniques—rituals—that
attempt to synchronize the three dances, the personal, the
cultural, and the cosmic. If the technique works, the reward is
a new dimension of rhythm and time—the sacred.*

—Mickey Hart

Rhythm is a repeating pattern of beats marking the passage of time. It's
embodied in the very cycles of Nature: of life and death, evaporation and
rain, the sequencing of ocean waves and tides, the inhalation and exhalation
of animal breath, the donning and shedding of leaves. Earth is a planet heavily
influenced by the recurrent phases of an orbiting moon, and is dependent
upon and defined by its steady pace around the sun. The consistent heartbeat
of the mother is the first sound a fetus hears afloat in the womb, and a child
is born into a rhythmic world. In a sense, the health of an individual or ecosystem is the result not only of its diversity, but the polyrhythmic interaction
of its constituent parts. Taking this metaphor a step further, it's as though,
through its practiced separativeness, civilized humanity has gotten "off beat,"
out of synch with the overall composition of greater creation.

Rhythm can be an aide to reconnection, and the drum is an instrument of
rhythm. Drumming has the potential to lead both the player and the engaged
audience into deep sensory and emotional contact with their natural selves,
each other, and the natural world of which they are an integral part. Played
rhythms can reflect and, at times, entrain with the rhythms of the body, sus-
pending normal cognition and intellection, and leading to an expansive feeling of connection or oneness. The result may be not only musical, but magical.

For the practitioners of New Nature Spirituality, as for "primitive" indigenous peoples, the meaning and success of human affairs is held to be
determined by natural spirits and forces. The drum is a vehicle for the Shaman to access the realms of these spirits, in order to bring back to the people
the wisdom and songs found there. The medicine elders of many tribes and
traditions—such as the Inuit of Canada, the Hourani of Ecuador, and the

Siberian Buriat—employ distinct mesmerizing rhythms for the purpose of encouraging an altered, hyper-intuitive state that can lead to sacred visions, heroic spiritual assignments, or miraculous cures.

Drums produce the low frequency "steep fronted" sonic impulses that most strongly affect the auditory cortex. Interestingly, experiments in the field of biofeedback have determined that the psychically aroused "alpha/theta border" occurs when the electric brain waves are pulsing at a rate of six to eight cycles per second—the predominate tempo of Haitian Voodoo music and African trance dancing. The theta state occurs after sex and right before sleep: the twilight phase when linear thought succumbs to free-form images, and awareness of the narrowly defined self is supplanted by identification with the shifting fields of an organic Whole.

Drumming and ecstatic dance are common elements not only of primitive land-based tribes, but also of many contemporary gatherings featuring a synthesis of spirituality and Nature, including Eugene, Oregon's Environmental Law Conference, the annual Earth First! Rendezvous, the Rainbow "tribe" get-togethers in the United States and Europe, and Pagan festivals such as Starwood in New York or the Solstice and Equinox events at Stonehenge in Great Britain.

> *...multitudes of Negroes of either sex make their barbaric beats*
> *and the sound of many and horrible congas, dancing*
> *dishonestly, immorally and singing gentile songs....*
> —Bernardo Vilhena

The drum's purported ability to provoke personal religious experience was understandably threatening to various state churches and their far-flung missionaries, as was its tendency to excite behavior the Christianized Roman Empire ruled "licentious" and "mischievous." Portuguese colonizers in Brazil in the 16th and 17th centuries enforced laws against the percussive music of their African slaves. The sound of Native American drums was sometimes enough to trigger a violent response from the U.S. Cavalry during the messianic religious revival of the late 1870s, which is known to historians as the Ghost Dance. Since the 1960s, drums have been a regular feature of environmental protests throughout the world, from efforts to save the Daintree forest in New South Wales, Australia, to "drum-ins" at the Nevada nuclear test site. Ecoactivist drummers include Starhawk, who is an acclaimed author and Wiccan priestess known for her community organizing and environmental stance.

The styles of drums range from tiny Asian finger drums to the giant hanging barrel drums found in various Buddhist temples in Japan. Some have one head, others are covered at both ends. Handheld open-frame styles were popular with Siberian Shamans as well as the Druidic priests of ancient Great Britain. The most popular handmade drums in America today are designs that originated in Africa: the narrow-bottomed ashiko, and the hourglass-shaped djembe. Until the introduction of the first plastic heads in the 1950s, drums were built entirely of natural materials. Their womb-like shells were usually constructed of wood or clay, with heads made from animal skin stretched tight with the help of iron bolts and rings, or with cord laced at the sides.

The carvers of ceremonial drums take into account the religious symbology of the materials with which the drums are made. The bodies of the instruments may be sculpted into the shapes of animal spirits, dyed with sacred minerals or shed blood, or hung with fur and feather. In Cuba, as late as the 1860s, priests of the Abakua brotherhood are said to have used drums made out of human skulls during their funeral rites, alongside symbols of resurrection. In ritual terms, the impermanence of life is made more bearable through the apparent impermanence of death.

Other traditional percussion instruments employed for ceremonial and spiritual purposes include rattles, shakers, gongs, bells, claves (wood blocks), the African m'bira (thumb piano), and the Brazilian berimbau (a wire affixed to a wooden bow, struck with a painted stick, and with a coin eased against the wire to effect a haunting vibrato). In the creation of rhythms, the player becomes a part of a process that goes back to the very beginnings of time.

"A sound precipitates air, then fire, then water and earth," Joseph Campbell wrote, "and that's how the world becomes. The whole universe is included in this first sound, this vibration...."

And as we came, so shall we go.

Both our fullest enjoyment of our mortal years, and the very survival of the human species may hinge on this one thing: our purposeful re-entrainment with the rhythms, cycles, processes, and needs of the greater living world. So gather the drums! With every shake of our rattles, we're embedded deeper...in the Gaian composition, the music and the magic, the direction and the dance...the drumming circle of life!

Forward, then. Forward in the rhythm.

A good cook is like a sorceress who dispenses happiness.
—Elisa Schiaparelli

There's an element of magic in cooking. And a loving cook is a magician.

Magic, after all, is the spell behind every successful recipe. No matter how basic its designs or mundane the presentation. No matter how often it's been served or how quickly consumed...and it's one of the missing ingredients in any culinary flop. The element of sorcery is evident to the guests of the Earthen Spirituality Project, especially when they are in the lovely host Loba's kitchen, wide-eyed in the presence of a flaming glaze flambé at midnight. Or ushered into a state of enchantment by the designs of foodstuffs artfully arrayed on the plate, their colors swimming about under the influence of allspice and candlelight. There's certainly magic afoot whenever sunlight does that ol' soft-shoe across the drying dishes. Whenever Loba leans toward the window facing the river, to better spoon moonbeams into the blueness of her bowl. And when an eagle calls, just as the cook concludes her daily dinner's blessing. Watch her lift a spatula in the air like a magic scepter, followed by a trail of tiny exploding stars. A gentle motion of her hand, and Loba calls forth the spirit of flying doves from a steaming pot pie, evokes the essence of laughing children residing in homemade cookies and milk, raises swaying sheaves of wheat from the holy ground of her wholesome crusty bread.

Not that the essence of the magical is restricted to such singularly exquisite moments. There is utter magic in the way that organic molecules reconfigure themselves, making the transition from soil to plant, to animal and to human, and inevitably back to soil again. There's magic in our digestive systems, a partnership of bodily acids and bacteria rendering food into a puree of assimilable nutrients. In the way smells transport us through an ether of mirage-like memories and immediate desires. The way that tiny single-celled yeast plants inspire bread dough to heave and rise. The way that the sun's rays are swallowed up by the glistening leaves, sweetened with the tree's best intentions, and then squirted into the chambers of a pulsing orange: The effects of the orange on our tongue. The bodily mending made possible by its vitamins and its minerals. The inevitable smile on the face of any kid who eats it.

A magic potion is that which enchants and charms, inducing a state of heightened perception, raising the sensation of smells and tastes to a fevered pitch. It dissolves the line between excruciating awakeness and sensuous sleep, daytime visions and nighttime dreams. They say it only takes one dusting from the fairy godmother's silk box, or a splash of holy water, or a drink from the sacred ram's horn...for the heart and senses to overcome the rational mind. A single bite of one of Loba's meals, and mighty revelations thunder in. A connection with the universe is made. Great things are suddenly possible, and yet there is nowhere one needs to go...all that matters is right here.

Indeed, a hush always seems to come over the room whenever Loba, the "Loving Cook," serves our meals. Perhaps it's the momentous arrival of the artfully displayed food that quiets the anxious chatter, bewitched by the stunning colors and mesmerizing smells. Or it could be the way that Loba makes her welcome deliveries: Walking in like a princess. Bowing like a servant. Hovering like an angel. Smiling like a fairy who has just this minute made everyone's wish come true!

We stare at the bowls being carefully placed one at a time in front of every favored diner. With forks, tongs, and ladle, the Loving Cook assumes her place at the head of our wooden table. We glance up at her arrival, then look one after the other into our fellow devotee's eyes...and sigh. To "consecrate" means to make sacred through our acts, our efforts. Thus, when we reach out and grasp hands, it is a moment of deliberate, wordless consecration, forming an ancient circle suspended in time. Centuries seem to pass by, the steam wafting upwards like holy incense. Through the aromatic mists of these heaven-bound clouds, a gentle voice rings out:

"Thank you, food, for giving yourselves to us. And for bringing us together in gratitude."

Loba's prayers are often short, and always to the point! What folks call "saying grace" also means acknowledging grace, and *exhibiting* grace.

"Thank you, Great Spirit, for a full bowl, an empty belly, and a willing heart!"

With words like these, the Loving Cook turns to kiss me, and all hands part to grope and gather the food upon our platters. Little is heard besides the clink and scrape of forks, and those irrepressible little "Yums!" Once again, as nearly every day of our lives, the inspirited Earth provides.

It is said, "Give us this day, our daily bread." We can think of food as manna from heaven—but it's manna we should strive to be worthy of nonetheless. Food tends to teach its own set of seven cardinal virtues: the humility and hope of hunger, the dedication of the gardener or gatherer, the wisdom that comes with intimacy with Nature and engagement with elemental necessity, the sensuality of the enlivened taster, the discernment of the cook, the compassion that follows food's call to share, and the gratitude of the wholly fed. And among the many other ways, a person is made deserving through their love and response, their veneration and commitment, the intensity and sincerity of their devotions.

The Loving Cook turns every aspect of her life into a mindful, prayerful practice. She's ever conscious of the source of our food, giving thanks with every breath to the fertile, hallowed ground. Thanks to God, to Gaia, to the Holy Spirit in any language, by any name. She understands that the quality of "holiness" is related to "wholeness": being complete, coherent, connected through Spirit to all that is.

For tens of thousands of years, on all parts of the globe, food was held sacred. Sacred not just because we required it to live, but because we recognized in it an expression and bodily extension of the divine Whole. Food appeared as a tangible manifestation of the *Anima Mundi,* the world soul. In fact, for most of our long history, humans believed that to consume life of any kind was literally to "eat God," to consume and assume the manifest flesh of Spirit: a pantheon on a plate! To the ancestors of every race, a feast was a ritual partaking of the *agape,* the sacred meal. They likewise affirmed the intrinsic wholeness/holiness in every element of unperverted Nature. They recognized that the most integrative and satisfying truths in life come not as rational conclusion, but as spiritual revelation, as *epiphany.* They knew—as we are obliged to learn—a ritual approach to our dinners that heightens meaning while deepening sense of value: Every meal, a magic rite. Every food, a source of connection.

There was a time in the not so distant past when all devotional rosary beads were made out of real rose petals, hand rolled and sealed with lampblack. Instead of tasteless communion wafers, the priests served real and wholesome chunks of bread, broken from a common loaf. Wiccans make their ceremonies more real by hand feeding each other bread and mead. It is this depth of authenticity, relevance, and nourishment that empowers any genuine religiosity—"binding together." Handling, smelling, and eating of the same foods binds us in exquisite experience as well as corporal purpose. We bond with the food, with the earth that supplies it, with the gentle hands that planted or fed or transported it. We bond with one another through shared experience and shared tastes. We bond with our families, our communities, and our ecosystems; bond with all that is.

Watching Loba prepare food is a lesson in the spiritual dimensions of cooking. She appears as an acolyte—her kitchen counter an altar loaded not just with artfully rendered foods, but kitchen implements invested with the intent and magic of important ritual tools. She presides over a bountiful table, from the ecumenical appetizers to her finger-bowl ablution. She serves as cantor, leading the congregation in joyful song, earning the blessings of the muses. She functions as pastor as well as baker. As seer, soothsayer, Shaman, and sage. As an unrenounced nun, in frilly apron habits. Loba is a zealot, a true believer, a sheep in the fold of pastry dough. She's a missionary of glad tidings and purple grapes seeking aesthetic and spiritual redemption for fast-food infidels, while offering comfort and support to any fellow cooks who have lost their way. Hers is a service with servings, a ministry of morsels. An assignment. A true calling she has little choice but to heed—eyes a-sparkle, mouth watering.

No matter how modern or mundane, every kitchen in the world offers an opportunity for revelation: self-knowledge, self-love, empowerment, connection, and enchantment! Learning to prepare and relate to food is no chore, but rather a rite of passage, a test that no one else can take for us, a sacred quest for the reclamation of our own sentient souls. Cooking opens the door and invites us into the experience of sacred space. We can each rise from the womb of the kitchen as from a birthing hut. Our fears and illusions, hesitation and self-doubt are all that gets in the way of our being forever altered by this mealtime litany: re-formed into our original selves, revealed as responsible celebrants of miraculous life, as agents of Gaian process, as playmates and vehicles for omnipresent Spirit! As cooks, eaters, and committed praise-givers!

Let us open our mouths to new tastes, our minds to new ideas, and our hearts to love. And let us open our eyes wide...to the day-to-day miracle of our numinous lives.

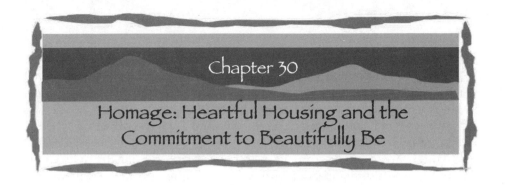

Chapter 30

Homage: Heartful Housing and the Commitment to Beautifully Be

We belong to the ground, it is our power and we must stay close to it; or maybe we will get lost.

—Yirrkala, Aborigine

In beauty we walk.

—traditional Navajo prayer

I love this area not only because there is a minimum of human habitation, but because many of the structures in this rural county reflect the history and character of the land. Mud bricks and clay tiles on a frame of vega logs and woven branch latillas. So many other places I go there seems to be a cancer of construction, with characterless tract homes and institutional-looking apartment buildings. They are oppressive in their sameness, the endless look-alike squares on look-alike streets in Anywhere, America. It is enough to raise the hunger for open space, in the way that roaring jets, sirens, and gunfire can increase our thirst and need for silence. On the other hand, some housing grows out of the land like landscape, like caves, like trees. We unfold within them, and they within us.

I'm particularly enamored with the oldest and most archaic of homes, as meaningful and inspirited as the ordered rocks of Stonehenge or the stark exposed walls of American Indian ruins. They often feel like little monasteries, places of refuge, the destinations of Spirit-minded pilgrims, the abode of heart. Gingerbread houses for enchanted grandmothers, with gardens for fairies and their glad-hearted fans. Once inside some hallowed old house, it seems like we can feel the various moods, the emotions of the individuals of past generations. Whether an East Coast townhouse with its basement and attic, or a moss-covered log cabin in Oregon, I experience a "take off your hat and lower your voice" humility when first entering one. The sense is of the hand work in each board and brick, and the investment of so many human hours into living within its fastened frame. Polished oak floors glisten with the tears of joy and anguish as much as polish, brought to a deep luster by sliding stocking feet, tongue-and-groove boards reflecting the busy shifting images of families growing, dying, changing. The fence rails absorb more than the sweat of hands tender and strong, teasing and anxious—little hands reaching up, crippled hands working for a grip. They soak up and then exude the over-lapping emotions of resistance and resignation, engagement and denial, loss and gain, love and anger, desire and satisfaction. Take out the heavy wooden furniture and the dark floral drapes, the heavy woolen rug and the leaded glass light fixtures hanging from the center of the ceiling, bring in bright acrylic pile and trendy aluminum-edged lithographs, but an old house will still re-verberate with the echoes of the past. One can repaint, but something deep and old continues to shine through. Some walls give the impression they're imprinted with intricate shadows cast by yesteryear's window lace. Another holds a stranger's attention the way it had when it hosted that oval-framed tintype, featuring the roving eyes of the scowling family patriarch.

Ask yourself what sort of people lived in the house you're in right now, before you ever did. Were children born in its back rooms, were there proud matriarchs who breathed their last breath where the sun still comes in the east window? The house may be new, or you may be the apartment's first tenant, but were there structures torn down to make room for the one you moved into? Perhaps a row of old uninsulated brick houses scraped aside for a new development, or a flat-roofed adobe casita given way to ranch houses with large windows and Kentucky bluegrass lawns? The ethnography of one neigh-borhood may have changed several times over the course of the last 200 years, from Indian to Spanish and French, French to English, an Italian quarter now considered part of the Cuban enclave, extended Irish families supplanted by Afro-Americans, in turn replaced by buyers of diverse racial backgrounds who by chance or fortune can afford the rising cost of its real estate.

Look outside. What people tended gardens in the bottoms, on the con-stant lookout for raiders, and were these "raiders" the peoples they were encroaching on? What indigenous tribe once gathered shellfish from the edge of the bay and walked the narrow trail where the interstate now lies? And who preceded them? I live in a river canyon uninhabited for a thousand years before I got here. But a few miles away, the river winds through a valley where the trailers of retirees sit amongst baked mud haciendas, the residents of the latter keeping alive much of the traditional Hispanic, frontier lifestyle. I love watching a family roast their chilies, the oldest son off to hunt for the winter's meat, the little girls braided with bows for the many fiestas. From where I park our truck to walk into our place, I can see the land that be-longed to Senovio, our deceased *patron,* or protector. The little casita is as empty as a torn pocket, and the status-earning satellite dish he never even used is now nearly hidden by a curtain of beautiful, uncut weeds. But I re-member that land as an extension of the little man with the big straw hat. When I look over that way, I imagine the way he looked at the sharp crack of

dawn, leaning on a pitchfork, pointing with pursed lips at the horses fill-
ing up on their breakfast hay. His beloved animals were fed, and the sun
was up in its usual show of morning color. I see the silhouette of this
Spanish American with the baggy pants, rooted to his place, contemptu-
ous of any cities more than a three-hour drive from his needy animals,
doubtful of or indifferent to any claims of distant wonders. Everything he
ever wanted, everything that mattered, was closer than that. Close enough to
see, maybe close enough to smell, certainly close enough to nod at, slowly,
with a tip of a dusty Stetson hat.

But there is more. Behind him, camped beneath the cottonwoods or sneak-
ing up on him from behind the barn, I sense the intrepid Apache. And behind
them, the pit-house and cliff-dwellers they preyed on, the ancestors of the
Pueblo Indians, the people they call "the Old Ones" pushing corn seed into
the riverside soil with a willow stick. They are the earliest known human
inhabitants of this bioregion, and their presence can still be felt more than a
thousand years after their migration away from this river drainage. In countless ruins, in the remnant stone-age irrigation ditches, in the cliff art and
pottery sherds scattered about the desert floor, in the multihued vistas they
themselves fancied—here we find the legacy of the Sweet Medicine People.
To archaeologists they are known as the San Francisco Culture or the Basket
Makers, and are commonly but mistakenly referred to as the Anasazi (a Navajo word originally meaning "the enemy"). And before, yes, *before* a single
human foot edged across this rain-licked rimrock, there were those other
intrinsically wild beings, plants, and animals characterizing and being characterized by the interplay of elements and energies that is land, in the unique
combinations that define the land. Behind the Hispanic elder's silhouette are
the shadows of the Apache and the echoes of the Old Ones. We see, we feel,
we delight in the dancing ghost images of leaf and tendril, tail and paw, fin
and feather fluttering in the dawn breeze, sensuously rubbing up against a
New Mexico sky.

On the way to town, I pass adobes still standing after 150 years, and log
cabins with clever cisterns to catch the sparse rainfall. And in the mountains
we find recently erected houses that look as though they're grown out of the
earth itself, resplendent with magical gardens, nested with purpose and grace,
built by a new generation of courtesans and celebrants of the land. Old or
new, regional, ceremonial, and owner-built structures can be embodiments
of what it means to give "homage": honoring self, Earth, and Spirit through
the artful and ecologic co-creation of human and home. In the acreage between the houses are masses of drought-tolerant wildflowers. They, like we,
are hearty examples of reinhabitation—an embodiment of billions of years
of history, promised to beauty, and committed to beautifully be.

Chapter 31

Mother Gaia

Gaia theory is as out of tune with the broader humanist world as it is with established science. In Gaia we are just another species, neither the owners nor the stewards of this planet. Our future depends much more upon a right relationship with Gaia than with the never-ending drama of human interest.

—James Lovelock

Our complex physiology begins with a single fertilized zygote cell ecstatically splitting into two, and then diversifying to fill all the roles of a functioning organic system. And just as the cells of our body are related, organized, and cooperative, so, too, all living and so called "non-living" things in Nature work together harmoniously for the health, diversity, manifestation, and fulfillment of the contiguous Whole. We are relatives, organs, and extensions of that vital Whole we're calling Gaia. Gaia hungering in heat. Gaia carrying the seed and substance of every imaginable potential. Gaia giving birth to herself.

I spend perhaps all too much time on this laptop, trying to spread messages of insight and affirmation to any who will read them. Sitting Buddha-like on my busy desk is Oberon Zell-Ravenheart's sculpture "The Millennial Gaia," which serves to remind me of the ways I *am* the Mother Earth, expressing herself through the devotions of heart and hand. From her head fall braids of twisted DNA, on the arterials of which every manner of ancient and contemporary life dance and climb. Her belly is the swollen globe, a fertile womb heavy with promise. It is she to whom every thing and being is born.

ArchWizard Oberon's Gaia figure is but one of the finer of Earth Mother images, and one of the latest in an ancient lineage of hand-carved reverence and respect. The well-known Willendorf Goddess, or Venus of Willendorf, was carved from bone in Europe some 32,000 years ago, and was long held to be the oldest verifiable human artifact. But as Amber K of Ardantane brought to my attention, a very similar Mother figurine recently discovered in the

Golan Heights of Israel has been carbon-dated at between 232,000 and 800,000 years old! This Acheulian Goddess, with her milk-laden breasts and divine vulva, predates the Willendorf by an astounding quarter million years! This sets the date for the beginnings of human culture—and by inference, the earliest worshipping of the Blessed Mother, the sacred feminine—back to the very roots of human experience...to the Paleolithic itself!

To quote Homer, she is "the eldest of all, and mother of all the Gods." She is the embodiment of Spirit in this section of the universe, and thus the Source and Wellspring for all primal religion. It is she who inspires the founders and informs the practitioners of every ecocentric spiritual practice—including Wicca and Wizardry, pantheism and Neo-Paganism, Deep Ecology and Druidry. No matter what we call ourselves, Gardnerian, Universalist, Eclectic, or Voudou...Gaia is the source of our beings and the venue for our visions. Mothers don't need to compete for attention with the other gods and goddesses, for they are her children, and of her. She is the mother to whom all seekers can turn for encouragement and direction, and her dreams can bring clarity, focus, and power to every form of spiritual and magic practice. And for everyone, even those who deny or dishonor her, she is the lap and cauldron we tumble back into when we die...the flesh and the prayer from which we arise.

Depending on the tongue, she is Mother Earth, Cybele, Mami Aruru, Nu Kwa, or Terra. She is known as Assaya in Yoruba, Kunapipi to the Aborigines, the Hindu say Prithivi...and to the indigenous people of Peru she is Pachamama, from whose body we sprout and grow like limbs or appendages. In the Greek version she is created from light and love out of the encompassing chaos. Her first-born was Ouranos, the heavens. Fertilized by the energies of Eros, she bears the many influences and spirits we call gods and goddesses, as well as the continents and oceans, the animals and plants...and us. To all cultures in touch with the natural world, any attempt or tendency towards separation would deny us the blood and nourishment of the Earth, and thereby ensure our doom. Even to neglect or ignore her, and our connection and duties to her, is felt to be enough to bring us the dis-ease of civilization and the attendant environmental crisis.

There are at least two indications of a wholly involved and dynamic community: When some ensure that there's an investment to purchase and resacrament land for ritual and healing. And when there is a succession and overlap of like-hearted, like-directed generations—when children are born into the extended family with the support of elders, and with a community school or other provisions for teaching the tribe's children in the ways of Earth and Spirit. I recently found myself captivated by the sight of my friend

Dee Reid's swollen belly as we attended an Albuquerque Solstice event called the Long Dance. Near term, she looked the epitome of Gaia. One could see in her countenance every emotion from empathic suffering to unbridled ecstasy, and from the urgency of our mission to the contentment that is our reward. Her mate, Ezra, cozied up to her the way creation clings to and cuddles with the sexy and motherly Earth. And Dee appeared as a promise more than a symbol, a commitment to give of herself as Gaia gives of herself again and again. In this time of overpopulation and escalating threats, making babies isn't and shouldn't be for everyone. And yet there are few ways of making our lives and practices more real than bearing or supporting the bearing of children into a Gaia-loving tribe.

While I sadly seldom see my own offspring anymore, their essence is stamped on my being, as ours is imprinted on the clay soul of the Earth. I was fortunate to be there, and to be the only one there when it came time to receive two of them. I'll never forget the way their mamas, like all expectant mothers, seemed to embody a Gaia willing to hurt to give life. I can still picture the sweat on their brows, like the clouds that hug the top of the canyon's cliffs, and then drip off it's flesh-toned sides. The heaving of the abdomen like arching lions mating, like mountains being born. The stretching or tearing of the holy cave, and that wonderful smell!—the smell of saltwater, the smell of Gaia's uterine seas.

The umbilical is cut, but the connection never severed. Each infant is fed by the energies and examples of Gaia in all her forms and shapes. Each grows into an adolescent with the choice to treasure or disdain what the young child once felt and knew, and yet Gaia will speak to them still. And as adults facing those dark pivotal moments of terror and disorientation, it will be some face of Gaia, in whatever leafy or fleshen guise, that turns them back into balance with the light. Those that consciously stay close to her throughout, or who courageously return to her embrace, are the assigned Wizards and Witches of a new/old way—Gaia's way. Whatever rites they cast their circles for, whatever cloaks they wear, they step forth as her glad and purposeful children— her babies, her suitors, her champions, her love.

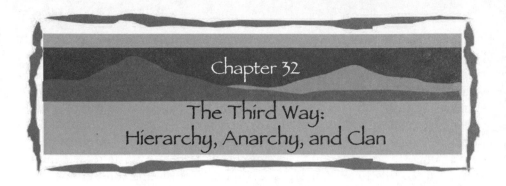

Chapter 32

The Third Way:
Hierarchy, Anarchy, and Clan

Sometimes there is confusion that the tango is the steps. No.
Tango is the feeling. It is one heart and four legs.

—Juan Carlos Copes

Government and Politics

The word *politics* is derived from the Greek *politikos*, meaning "of a citizen." As such, politics is simply the affairs of the common man/woman, the ways in which we determine the affairs of our kind. But at its root we discover "polis," the city. With this we're reminded how politics is first and foremost the province of the ruling cities, and with few exceptions does great harm to the disenfranchised: the conquered and exploited, the women and youth, the yeomen and farmers of the countryside...and the entire natural world existing just outside the town limits and castle walls.

So the question of our time becomes: how do we manage our collective selves in ways that are personally empowering and Earth-honoring? How do we enjoin the politics of interrelationship, without certifying historic systems known for destruction and lies? Certainly the option to participate is voluntary, and should be conditional as well. We should decide when to involve ourselves and when not to, weighing each situation, the possible effect we might have on a situation, and effect that this involvement will have on us.

Government is the institution of politics. To govern means not only to exercise political authority, but also "to direct and restrain; to control the actions or behavior of." We look to our political and judicial leaders to keep polluters from poisoning American estuaries or to punish the multinational logging companies driving hundreds of plant and animal species to extinction. Some of the most impressive environmental gains over the past few decades have been political, our victories mostly legislative or litigious. But by appealing to the central authorities, we validate the power of the same institutions that support profit-making logging companies driving one species after another into irretrievable extinction, that colonize the labor force of undeveloped third-world countries, and codify the "right" to pave over nearly every inch of living soil in the name of "progress." And every environmental judgment or legislation can be just as easily reversed or repealed according to the whims of an ever-expanding population. Increasingly, one of the fundamental choices for all political participants will be between setting aside space for the evolving natural world, and its appropriation for human habitation and use. Kudos to every activist and group who have been able to turn the system against itself, Aikido fashion, and won for even a single generation or single decade a reprieve for the threatened forests and retreating wildlife. But any long-term remedy—any lasting return to balance—will require more than the always temporary support of the judicial and political process.

The Problem With Systems and the Appeal of Anarchy

In the 1960s, there was an ideology that rather than opposing the dominant paradigm, we had only to build healthy alternative infrastructures (communities, schools, food co-ops, spiritual traditions) and then watch Babylon crumble all around us. Only problem is, Babylon is flourishing, and may continue to do so long after the killing off of a large percentage of "higher" life forms, the draining of the last oil reserves, and the soiling of the air and sea. Humanity will likely have the technological ingenuity and *political will* to outsurvive almost everything except for microbes and cockroaches...at the expense of every other living thing.

Fortunately, the alternative structures we built have survived as well, if only as the rekindled dreams and manifest expressions of an Earth-loving, peace-loving minority. And at the same time, there continues to exist a countercurrent of thoughtful outcasts, serving as a kind of antidote to the system's suffocating order...calling themselves anarchists, calling themselves *free*.

In its extreme, anarchy makes for an indulgent personal credo, and a dysfunctional and uncooperative society. But it's no wonder that kids find the anarchic emphasis on individual expression, motivation, and responsibility preferable to the systemologies that have so long governed our kind. When people are in touch with their personal needs, or connected to the needs and will of the living Earth, they can no longer condone the monotony of colorless communism, the hierarchical absolutism of even the most noble kingdoms, or even that consumerist dictatorship of the masses we call "democracy." Every better-organized system known to "man" commodifies, trivializes, or totally eliminates individual liberty. They demonstrate the kind of artless rigidity that turns outlaws into mythical heroes, civil disobedience into a rite of passage, and nonconformity into a meaningful life quest. They insult our true human nature, while at the same time they manage and implement the destruction of the natural world.

It seems that no governing system has ever been immune. Even tribalism has a history of formalizing some less than Spirit-honoring practices, from the sanctioned wife beating of certain Native American societies, to the institutionalized human sacrifices of my own tribal Celtic ancestors. Tribal unity and survival are dependent on change-resistant traditions. These traditions are unwritten laws, alternately supported and believed in, resented and subverted, or blindly obeyed. And like all practice and law throughout our history, some have contributed to the health and diversity of natural ecosystems, while others have led to their destruction. In every tribe, as in every political system, the outcasts are those who seem fated to recognize the harm in tradition and law, the bards who must then communicate it, and the outlaws who must resist it.

A Third Way

It's crucial that we continue to imagine and work toward a more organic system of human interaction: one that exceeds the most positive examples of our primal forebears, while reviving those spiritual sensibilities once common to us all.

There is what I call the "Third Way," a model neither anarchic nor hierarchic: the archaic *clan*. A clan is first and foremost a coven of shared intentions, practices, priorities, and values. It is, by necessity, smaller than other societies, with people naturally breaking off and going their own ways when the group starts to get much more than 30 members. Decisions and duties naturally fall on those most obviously informed or gifted in each different circumstance. Often this will be a sage, elder, or crone—but on occasion it may be a child instead, who has shown the necessary understanding in the particular area of consideration. In every case, it falls on the shoulders of the one most able and willing to give and to serve—motivated by love, empowered by their connection to the All. Leaders are those who inspire others by their example.

Nobody is disadvantaged or suppressed when the group is so small that everyone can come to an agreement! In a healthy world (a world of vast wilderness), in order to disagree or diverge, one has only to leave, crossing over the mountains to join another clan, or to start one's own. Thus a clan was always held together not only by need and necessity, but by true affection and demonstrable loyalty. To this day, the voluntary members of any clan share not only common beliefs, but an overriding allegiance to their mutual good. They haven't had to learn to be a "more tolerant" society, *because they care about each other.*

Legal ownership of our Sweet Medicine Sanctuary property has proven to be a useful tool, but ultimate engagement and guardianship have been more the result of the devotion of clan. From the time I got here I sensed the clanhood of the Mogollon Mountains pit-house dwellers that took care of this river canyon thousands of years before us, and how we can best further this legacy of protection and sacrament with our own focused grouping. Folks that came and left each contributed in some way to the preservation of place. And those that have stayed contribute to the strength of our efforts, and the promise of a lineage: Wonder-filled Loba, singing prayers to the sacred cliffs, stroking the grass, kissing every rock and skull. Resident interns and apprentices, open to all there is to learn, gladly shouldering the Kokopellic burdens, giving their all in the most committed and creative ways. And our nonresident extensions, aiding this place and project while remaking their lives in the image of their dreams. We are united by the commitment to give everything we can, and to pay any price, for that which matters most.

In such a clan, common priorities and aims substitute for governance, and the mechanics of control are replaced by politics of empathy, commitment, devotion, and love.

*I have seen that in any undertaking it is not enough for a man
to depend simply upon himself.*

—Lone Man (Teton Sioux)

Nature serves as the context for any sustainable community whether
a grouping of people, or of other species. A spiritually, emotionally,
and physically healthy human society is impossible without an
awareness of, and a reciprocal relationship with, the larger, more-than-
human tribe.

Ecology is the study of interdependency among the innumerable elements
of a beautifully interwoven Whole. Impacting any single part will have un-
foreseeable effects on the rest, and one cannot understand any of the constituent parts outside of their greater context. Similarly, the ecology of
communities looks at the ways in which human societies interact with, are
influenced by, and depend on the nonhuman world.

You're likely familiar with those wooden Russian dolls that nest one inside the other. Take the top off one, and you reveal yet another doll inside,
again and again until uncovering the final, tiny seed doll. We can think of the
smallest doll as the self: the community of one's cooperative parts: organs,
skills, experiences, needs, and desires. Each part interacts with the rest according to its evolved purpose. This self-doll is nested in the larger human
community, which resides in and is linked to the fate of greater Nature.
Nature exists within a community of planets and stars, all of which are con-
tained by the forms and intentions of inclusive Spirit.

The process of remaking human society will require attention to the
diverse interests of our authentic inner selves. Both self and culture depend
on the sustenance and example provided by the natural world, and this natural
world requires our active protection. None of this is possible without the
inspiration and spark of life that is the gift of the sacred.

We have only to turn to our natural surroundings, our watershed and the wild animals that inhabit it, in order to come up with examples of balance and right living. We have only to turn outward, away from our preoccupation with emotional and material baggage, to tap the energy for an inspired reformation of our community soul.

At their best, our various social constructs both reflect and respond to the needs and patterns of the watersheds where they're situated. Traditionally, terrain, weather, and available natural materials dictate the type of structures characterizing a given community, such as the peaked roofs of Alaskan log cabins, and the flat roofs and thick, insulating walls of Southwestern adobe casas. For a glaring example of community indifference to the land it exists on and with/in, consider the bluegrass lawns and constantly evaporating swimming pools of desert suburbia. Little could be more obvious than the simple fact that arid regions require dry-land gardening strategies, and call for conscientious cactus and gravel landscaping.

Terrestrial and climatic influences also affect our activities, our schedules, and even our very characters. There's more at play than an easy stereotype when we speak about the "stoic" qualities of Midwestern farmers, their determination tempered by storm and crisis, their perspective shaped by flat lands and distant horizons, their patience a product of the empty miles between.

Even a modern city, filled with generic high-rises whose windows look out on nothing but other duplicate high-rises, demonstrates a palpable sense of character that's partially an effect of the rivers coursing through it, the ocean lapping at its beaches, or the mountains rising just out of sight. To some degree even the most insular and self-absorbed of societies must still feel it, and reel from it: the power of a blazing sun, the effect of long months of Northwest cloud cover, the muffled imploring of the earth beneath the pavement. Tactile rock, beating wing, and exploring, subterranean roots all touch the populace at the subconscious level. The angst and hope and inspiration that result surface in yearning arts, musical laments, and the primarily unanswered desire for us to feel at home.

On the other hand, a balanced, vibrant society consciously takes its cues from the natural world around it, and responds to the needs of that world as it provides for its own. It takes on the elements of local Nature as co-members of an intentional community, as pledged allies, and as lovers contributing to the well-being of the Whole, sensitive to matters that threaten its integrity or dilute its intensity of being. Such a society can be said to be ritually and fundamentally bedded in the adjoining natural world, as much as plants are bedded in the living soil. It is this essential, comprehensible ground-ing that affords us the wisdom of stewardship, and the grace for redemption.

The root of the word *community* is the Latin *communis*, meaning "com-mon." Other words growing out of the same root include: *commune*, the most deliberate sharing of contemporary social experiments; *communiqué*, which can include interspecies messages; and *communicate*, which literally means "to make common." A healthy society is bound together by what its residents and participants share in common: shared intentions, shared needs, a body of ideas affecting the ways that we live and the quality of that life.

Certainly this is no longer the case for most American urban centers. Financial opportunity has become the primary and often sole reason for people picking a particular place to live. The second most important criterion is usu-ally a comfortable home, followed by a "comfortable" neighborhood and avail-able recreational opportunities. All too seldom is the reason a desire to live near relatives or to die in the habitat of our personal family history. Or to be in the company of like-minded folks, engaged in that hard day-to-day work called "utopia." Or to answer a soul-deep call from the lap of the redwoods, the bosom of the Rockies, the heart of the Midwestern grasslands.

I speak not as a successful communard, but as one who has slipped through the fine cracks of the social screen, proposing a harmonic social body from which I myself have opted out. Even if I stumbled upon the functioning, Earth-centered tribe I've always dreamed of, I'd likely find myself making camp at the farthest edge. Like a seeker, or a Shaman, or a leper taking advantage of the stillness and the silence in order to apprehend the movement of power and the voices of the land!

I've been disgorged from the impersonal maw of one of this country's largest metropolises. I've even found it difficult to function happily in the cooperative folds of alternative community. I understand the essential value of consensus, while finding it outside my nature. I appreciate the highest ex-pressions of culture, but was born looking at them as if from afar. I've been too easily wounded by the back-fence gossip that helps sustain the fabric of even the most radical of alternative social experiments. In later years I prayed for, and did everything I could to orchestrate, the forming of clan and tribe around the protection and celebration of this bioregion, only to find that the land spit out all but the most die-hard, and that the folks we enlisted didn't always have the best effect on the land they came to live on.

While we need natural places for our survival, as well as for our deepest fulfillment and realization, if everyone spread out from the towns and vil-lages, there wouldn't be any undeveloped places left. No room for the plants and animals, no space for quiet, no arena for evolving wildness. No matter what my personal inclinations or failures, I know that the answer for our kind (in our times) is to cluster with like-minded folks in places we love, near those places we need. And to enter into communication with the nonhuman world as well as with one another, using what we learn in this cycle of touching and sharing to create a society to which we can be glad to belong.

Whether we're talking about a single family or the regional Pagan community, a small clan gathering around issues of social activism or an entire neighborhood or town...its survival, continuity, and effectiveness hinges on our cultivated ability to make common: recognizing the commonalities linking us to one another, linking our alliances and our fates to the cooperative association of the more-than-human realm.

Chapter 34

Reindigination: Primal Mind and the Responsibilities of Belonging

We see in the present best efforts of groups of non-Indians an honest desire to become indigenous in the sense of living properly with the land.

—Vine Deloria Jr. (Sioux historian)

in-dig-e-nous: adj. (1) Occurring or living naturally in an area; native. (2) Intrinsic, innate.

Our every magical and insightful power is a gift of Gaia, the Earth and her myriad reflective spirits—an outgrowth of our relationship and belonging. At the same time, people do not take as good of care of a place when they imagine they are only visiting. In this age of constant migration, the best hope for the suffering environment may lie in people of every race and culture settling down and committing to a place that speaks to them, heeding the imploring of its spirit and tending to its needs. The survival of myriad other species, and also the future of humanity, may hinge on the degree to which we are able to set aside our comfortable habits, preconceptions, and assumptions...and re-become conscious participants, discovering what it means to be native again.

Now more than ever we need to look to the remaining land-based tribal peoples, and to the qualities and possibilities of primal mind. Indigenous modes of perception become all the more essential as our modern society reels out of balance both ecologically and spiritually. The land-informed stories of indigenous populations can help us recover our lost awareness of self and place. The knowledge of how to live in balance, in a sustainable way, already exists...in the ways of the ancient ones of every continent. The information is all too often lost along with the unraveling of tribal customs, with time-tested skills and informed insights vanishing as fast as the lands appropriated for development. As our existence and enterprises become increasingly commercial and controlled, our pleasures ever more vicarious, our sense of both culture and place perverted or absent, as both our schedules and our thoughts race ever faster, we can still turn to those who have lived here and loved here the longest. Turn to the Native American elders, the placed peasants, the Hispanic dirt farmers with their knowledge of weather and wild foods, those nomads still following the reindeer and the seasons, the Kayapo and their jungle pharmacy. We must turn to them, not in order to emulate or simulate, but in a respectful search for the truths that are our birthright, for what it means to truly belong.

For all the differences in the worldviews and cosmologies of indigenous peoples, there are certain qualities they generally have in common. From one end of this world to the other, primal perception is likely to incorporate the following tenets:

- The Earth is alive, self-directed, with it's own primal consciousness.

- Life is inspirited and thus sacred with an innate, intrinsic value. The rocks and the lichen that feed on them, the trees and the rain that drips down them, all creatures and all people are vested with spirit, meaning, and purpose.

- All elements of the sacred Whole are interconnected, interdependent, and interrelated at the deepest levels...and all should be treated as our relatives. At the root of all personal and societal turmoil is the illusion of separateness, a dis-ease that must be guarded against from birth until death. Because there is no true "other," all beings are hurt by the dishonoring or degradation of any one.

- Humanity's additional cognitive abilities position us not above the rest of creation, but sorely in need of deliberate rituals to keep us grounded in relationship, purpose, and place. Our unique gifts were meant to result not in libertine distraction, but advanced responsibility. Our kind is called to attend to the needs and lessons of the natural world of which we are a part...to acknowledge, partake in, protect, and provide for the plants, animals, and waters that in turn nourish, instruct, inspire, and house us.

- Existence is to be smelled and tasted, embraced and absorbed. No words for food are meant to substitute for the benefits of eating...and all symbols and gestures are meant to bring us deeper into the actual wordless, physical, emotional, and spiritual experiencing of life.

◎ Everything in the world functions in part as a message, and all that happens to us, positive or negative, is potentially a valuable lesson. All truths and all beings are tested, and it is through these challenges that we earn our blessings, demonstrate our qualifications, validate our worth, and manifest our love.

◎ Spiritual knowledge or power requires the complete, painful dissolution of illusion and the fearful societal self...and a committed realignment and recommitment according to the designs of Spirit and place.

◎ Such designs exist for all things, heeding the imperatives of Gaian rhythm, pattern, and will.

◎ All things occur in cycles, and all energy and life seek to circle— to return to its migratory origins, to spin in the grass before settling down nose to tail. All that exists is an eternal now, rolling over in place like a salmon, exposing in turn each of its sides Summer to Fall, Winter to Spring, first night and then day. Human kind, too, turns in place, sequentially offering up the face of an anxious infant, a tempestuous teen, a focused adult, a grandfather or crone.

◎ The hero's quest moves toward and never away from authentic self and inspirited place, heightened awareness and applied magic, meaning and mission...a true journey home.

Primal mind isn't just for the Shamans and seekers of a few tribes, the tranced-out peoples of Ladakh, the Kogi, or the Shuar. It is, rather, a region or capacity of the instinctual human body, accessible by even the most predisposed of us. It surfaces during lovemaking, while crossing the slick head of a waterfall, in the presence of enraptured children, whenever circumstance and surprise have delivered us most fully into our sentient bodies. At these times, the Earth reveals itself as unquestioningly sacred, imbued with the numinous. Even the most mundane expressions of inanimate Nature appear alive, and one can sense movement in patterns of fiber and the grain of mineral and wood. We find ourselves in the timeless now, the eternal bodily and psychic engagement with the present, a part of an interconnected universe that unfolds and contracts in cycles. Even if only for the shortest period of time, we jettison words for reality, symbol for touch, and know the world through our primal minds. We feel more alive, complete, tested, and worthy. And we are. Honored to be. Honored to be here now.

We each become more indigenous to the degree that we reside in our primal minds, in place, in the bosom of the land, in the lap of the moment.

Becoming: coming to be, leaning how to really be, coming onto and into one's self. In re-becoming native, we re-create a contemporary culture, community, vocabulary, spiritual practice, and finally a history true to our mixed-blood ancestry and the urgent and trying times at hand. Along with our grounding comes an almost forgotten humility. We look to the first "two-legged" peoples to inhabit this continent for guidance, but we each must also establish our credibility directly with the land. We need to own our deepening connection, the fact that we, too, belong to the places we're promised to...even as we actively respect the ways of those peoples who showed respect to the land for so long before us.

In time we may come to recognize being native as a condition of relationship. Of sensitivity, engagement, reciprocity, and allegiance. To survive, those facing the tests of the next century will have had to learn to be placed. And they're likely to be of ever more mixed blood. They will be the descendants of Shona and Aborigine, Mongol and Semite, Hispanic and Cree, and they will have learned respect. They will be the proud inheritors of the affections of Aphrodite, the temperance of Chuang-Tzu, the resolve of Odin and Ogun, the determination of the Berserkers and the spirit of Crazy Horse. No matter where they're situate, they'll have survived because they came to know and manifest themselves, completely and unapologetically, as indigenous.

And this alone will have brought them a great peace.

Chapter 35

Truly Rich: Gaian Insight on Technology and Money

Deepness implies an attitude of dwelling in-the-moment, meditating, letting one's own rhythms and perceptual room open up; respecting and including what is there, what comes, involving the flow of actions from the level of the unconscious that Wilhelm Reich calls "Eros."

—Bill Devall

No matter what careers we choose—or what we ever do to make money—we really only have one job: the fullest actualization of our authentic beings...in service to each other, to divine Spirit and the living, feeling Earth. The technologies we employ should further our inhabitation of self and purpose in the here and now, assisting our sacred magical quests. In focused presence and purpose, sensation and service, we discover the meaning of rich.

Technology: Tool and Choice

We live in decidedly technological times, an age in which almost everything we do makes use of or is influenced by the wonders of industry and science. Being neutral in character, this powerful force can be used to create everything from important new medicines for AIDS to satellite surveillance and government mind control, from the long-lasting solar electric panels to nuclear blasts brighter than the sun. Brain implants can be used by doctors to help patients control their seizures, or by an intrusive world government that seeks complete control over our behavior. Because technology is a double-edged sword, we must try to be conscious of its effects on we who wield it. On the human psyche and the diversity of culture. On other species and greater environment. On the course of evolution and the manifest will of the inspirited Earth. It's relatively easy to call into question the accelerated development of weapons of mass destruction, or even much of the digital distraction that so often passes for home entertainment. But the implications and results aren't always so obvious.

A person grows stronger by pulling a load, pushing hard against an obstacle, or having a difficult mountain to climb. Thus by promising us ease and comfort, technology threatens to take away the very sources of our strength. It promises the possibility of us living hundreds of years through the use of synthetic bionic parts, and yet it is our awareness of the finite nature of life—of how relatively short our life spans are—that we come to fully appreciate, value, and concentrate on each precious present moment. It can accelerate our day-to-day activities and increase our production, but unless we take careful countermeasures, we may find ourselves experiencing things on a more superficial level, having no time for the depth of relationship and understanding that lead to wisdom and enlightenment. Because technology gives us the means to manipulate appearance, we find ourselves increasingly surrounded by the artificial, with a reduced capacity to know the difference.

The most "appropriate" technology, then, is that which uses up the least resources and does the least damage, while accomplishing the most good. Appropriate means not "efficient" so much as beneficial and beautiful—leading us not away from self, Earth, and Spirit, but ever deeper into the experiences we think of as "natural" or "spiritual." Likewise, the most "sustainable" technology is not the longest lasting, but that which helps sustain the spirit and dignity of human life, other life forms, our besieged environment, and this sacred planet Earth.

The laptop I write this on was created out of plastics made from oil, which contributes to the pressure for more drilling in sensitive places such as the pristine Arctic National Refuge. There's environmental damage and pollution associated with the production of its computer chips, and those hours spent on it writing about Spirit and the natural world are hours that could have been lived outside, directly engaged in the spiritual quest. Does this mean that those working to save the Earth and heal human kind should reject the latest tools of technology, leaving them to those who would manage or even destroy our planet home? Of course not. Nor should we ignore or deny the personal, social, and environmental damage caused by these tools. Instead, we can both compensate and make amends...by making the most of them, for all the best reasons. To justify their existence, to qualify their use, we need only to dedicate them to purposes that are generous enough, curative enough, beautiful enough.

When we are in touch with our magical selves, with Spirit and the will of the land, we naturally know which technologies to disuse or to use—and how. We are empowered by a sense of connection to the rest of enchanted Creation, impelled by a force deep inside us, committed to the real work of sustenance and significance, healing, and love.

The Meaning of Rich

Here is a personal story: As teenagers, we could already see how much of what folks called "being rich" came at the expense of old-growth forests and fragile wetlands, underpaid laborers in South Korea and the homeless huddling on America's streets. We liked to rant about "crass materialism," which we defined as "having more belongings and toys than free hours to enjoy them in." One day at a party aboard a Sausalito houseboat, the Zen sage Alan Watts set me straight on the term. He motioned me over, and asked me to feel the beautiful fabric of a hand-woven robe, the raised silk embroidery and deftly braided edges.

"A real materialist," he explained, "is someone who notices and relishes the actual material of this wondrous world." He took a slow sip of hot tea, smelling and savoring it, before beginning the task of making fillets of the night's salmon.

In the ensuing years I've come to realize there is nothing necessarily noble about being poor, nor is there anything special about having money. The poor are not always more grateful, nor does having a good income mean one is oblivious or uncaring. What's important is how rich we are in the things that matter most, how closely we pay attention to them, and how truly grateful we are!

I remember that even as a little boy I couldn't understand anyone with a big bank account and sad eyes. It hurt to watch them making up for a lack of self-love, or the absence of a personal mission, by buying more things. And it hurt worse to see them not really taking the time to daily appreciate the crafted wood and expensive fabrics they'd surrounded themselves with, not really taking pleasure in the many objects that they had bought.

So when does one have too many things? When we can't remember all that we have. When we have things we never use, things that have no sentimental meaning to us. When we can't take the time to learn its story and its history. When we can't find any way to use them to make our lives or the world a little more beautiful, a little more healed.

And when does one have too much money? When we have no other purpose for it besides easing our fears and insecurities about the future. When we seem to live to make money, giving all our time and focus to it, instead of making money in order to better live.

No matter what we may have heard, money isn't really the "root of all evil." It's just a symbol for the many uses that we put it to—whether it's spent on screwing things up or making them better, on making our immediate world uglier and lonelier or more wonder-full and caring. Money is most valuable to the degree that it provides us with a more meaningful and manifest life, useful for some greater purpose than simply our own personal survival and comfort. There are magical spells and practices to help attract money into our lives, but, most importantly, we need to find new ways of making magic happen with the money we have! As with any potentially magical energy, we have the option of gathering and hoarding it for personal gain or directing it for the betterment, balance, and bliss of all existence.

Without the strength of our intentions, cash is nothing but cold paper and shivering change. U.S. dollars are far too stiff to make rags, and don't burn well enough to start a lifesaving fire before the big hundred-year snowstorm hits. In other words, they have no real value outside of their ability to pay for real nourishment for our bellies and eyes, hearts and souls—to secure land, to fund a campaign for justice or wilderness, or to help us make dreams come true! Being rich, then, is never a matter of how much we have of anything. It's how much pleasure we get out of what we've got, how much these things deepen the significance of our lives, and how much good we do for others and for this Earth with what we make and own. Truly rich is the seeker who follows his heart, the teacher or child who does her part.

The very richest will always be those who give the most. And they will be richest in experience and purpose, in wisdom and understanding. In magical experiences and wild places. In compassion and truth, sensuality and meaning, family and tribe—in home, and in hope.

Chapter 36

The Return Home: Planting Seeds of Magic, Insistence, and Delight

In the course of human evolution, a change of mind, a new idea, can have as much survival value and adaptive significance as the mutation of a gene.

—Lyall Watson

There are more things in heaven and earth, Horatio, than are dreamed of in our philosophy.

—*Hamlet*, William Shakespeare

Author interviewed by Derrick Jensen, author of *A Language Older Than Words*, on July 8, 2000.

Derrick Jensen: Define home for me.

Jesse Wolf Hardin: Home is the feeling heart, in deep relationship with the land. And it is the place that calls us most insistently, instructs us loudest and best. The place we inevitably miss when we leave, partner to our pain, and reason for our joy. Home is not only where you want to live, but how you want to live. And the place where you want to be when death finally claims you.

To "lose our place" is to lose our way home.

Let me put it this way: the source of all psychological, social, and environmental dis-ease is our illusion of separateness. And the first step in mending that artificial schism—that deep and damning wound—is to try to bring ourselves back to a place of engagement with our authentic beings, in the vital present moment.

DJ: I don't understand.

JWH: The opening to the experience of the universe is through intimacy with a living planet, Gaia. The doorway to the experience of Gaia, is through our sentient animal bodies, and our feeling hearts. And the journey—the work, the realization—can only happen in immediate, present time. Reindigination begins with reinhabitation of our awakened bodies and roiling emotions, in the "now." Much of the natural world, and our own wild spirits, are dying as a direct result of our alienation and abstraction, from what I call our "great distancing." And perhaps most tragically of all, many of us are dying without having fully lived.

DJ: That reminds me of a quote you use from H.G. Wells: "One can go through contemporary life fudging and evading, indulging and slacking, never really frightened nor passionately stirred, your highest moment a mere sentimental orgasm, and your first real contact with primary and elemental necessities the sweat of your deathbed." What does this mean?

JWH: It's all too easy to acquiesce to the status quo, to the latest trends, and to our habits and fears. To give up our dreams for a meaningless career. To seek distraction in the television set and salvation in the sky. To compromise on a mate, and to pretend we're a victim of something called fate. To reside in the busy mind, and thereby avoid the pain of the neglected body and the anguish of an untended heart. To flounder around in the superficial rather than risk the frightening depths. To accept and acquiesce rather than discern and confront. To settle for comfort and safety instead of sensation and response-ability. We civilized humans are as tourists in our animal bodies except during certain moments in the midst of the sex act...or when scared for our lives. All too often, it's only when we face mortal or psychological destruction that we come back to the body that feels, runs, retaliates, or relieves. Back to ourselves, and back home.

Clearly social and environmental activism isn't enough, unless we can somehow change the way we as a species perceive and relate to the natural world, to land and place. We can claim all these small, short-term victories, but the fact is that the world is being deforested ever faster as we speak. More toxic chemicals are being released into the ground and water than ever. We're changing the climate. And genetic engineering poses what is perhaps the single greatest threat to the health and integrity of life on Earth.

DJ: Are we losing?

JWH: The trick to right relationship—and to really being worthy of this blessing called "consciousness"—is to do what is right, what matters most, regardless of the visible results. We seldom see the ramifications of all the good we do, but more importantly, we need to make the grand effort not because we imagine we'll succeed, but because it's right to do so. Because it really, deeply matters to us! And in a way, even discouragement and disgust are potentially good signs. They're evidence of an awareness of the odds stacked against us, and it is acting in spite of them that makes one's life heroic.

DJ: Are you saying results don't matter?

JWH: Of course they matter. But we watch for results in order to figure out the best actions to take, not for a reason to act. And sometimes we're able to accomplish the impossible. They call us magicians because what we do appears to defy logic and limitation. When the medicine man Crazy Horse saw his family and village under attack by the U.S. Army, he could see that the odds were stacked against him. In spite of this, he rode headlong into the fight, inspiring other braves to follow his example, and breaking the enemy ranks with the sheer intensity of his effort, his investment and risk, his life and love.

The important thing is to drop all expectations, which can lead to disappointment. And cling to hope, which is an empathetic prayer that we participate in, a seed we plant even if we never get to see the tree.

DJ: But we do. You see it all around yourself. You got the cows off of this land [Sweet Medicine Sanctuary], and the cottonwoods and willows have come back. It's beautiful.

JWH: It's protected for now, through sweat and threat, dumb luck and an essential assist from the spirits. And more than that, it's reveled in, honored, restored, and resacramented...and yet there are no guarantees. The best we can do is to wake up each and every day, giving thanks for being alive and aware in this enchanted place. Being who we really are, and doing everything we possibly can, for all the right reasons.

DJ: I'd like to go back to the notion of reinhabiting one's body. What are you saying?

JWH: Your door to the entire world is located where your feeling body touches the giving ground. Your bare feet, your rear end, the few square inches of absolute contact is point of connectivity between yourself and millions of years of organic process. And the way to fully experience that connection is by disengaging our mental tape loops, our voice tracks, the constant commentary that keeps us perpetually anticipating the future or criticizing our self about the past rather than tasting the muffin we're eating right now. Then we can experience the world around us—as well as within us—like the awakened, hungering, feeling, responding, caring creature selves we really are.

DJ: So reinhabiting one's body is tied intimately to reinhabiting the present moment.

JWH: We can't feel our connection to the sentient body, or participate in the processes of the natural world, anywhere but "here" and "now." And we can't really be either if we're forever residing in our brains, engrossed in the movies of our minds. All the while reality waves its arms and wings and cloud forms like flags trying to win back our attention, trying to give us back our lives. I mean, there's a reason why they call it the "present": because its a gift we're fools to miss.

Most of us have read that old science fiction classic where the professor departs his basement shop astride his "time machine," leaving nothing behind but a ring in the dust on the floor where it once stood. In the same way, civilized humanity is often out of touch, absent, unreachable by a world of unfolding presence. Our bodies remain in place like that impression in the dust, while our minds orbit backwards and forwards through the years, inhabiting every period of time but now, and every place but here. Too often we dwell on our desires and worries, rather than dwelling *in*—in the present, in place. And meanwhile, things such as industrial development and environmental destruction are largely accomplished out of time, by future-looking planners and bureaucrats who are oblivious to the purrs and the pleas, the rewards and challenges of the beckoning present. What we need is a conscious, collective high-dive into the always decisive moment—reimmersing ourselves in the sensations and responsibilities of the real world...now!

DJ: How does one begin to do that?

JWH: Reach out to what is real—a leaf, a chair, a friend—emissaries of the present glad to reconnect us to the now. If something exists for the senses, it exists in present time. Waking up from a nightmare of past events and faraway places, peer into the graduations of black in the unlit bedroom, focus on the pressure of covers against skin, or give yourself over to identifying any smells making their way to you through the darkness. Try showers hotter and colder than you think you can stand, focus on the lover you're with. And if all else fails, there's nothing like a loud boom, the sudden screeching of brakes, or a genuine near-death experience to bring us back into bodies ready to run or have fun!

There's so much distraction and obstruction, we have to remain fiercely focused and totally insistent. Because almost everything in society calls you away from yourself. The clamor and bright lights, standing in lines or working in offices, going to movies or making small talk. For the unplaced few, our society can seem like a very lonely place. The average Joe doesn't seem to want to smell as deeply or love as much. Or to risk deeply caring, 'cause it might mean he has to act on those things he sees and feels. Even the friends you've known forever might not affirm something that is a little bit heavier, a little deeper, than they may want to go. Maybe you becoming more of who you are mirrors something in themselves they don't want to deal with, and so they try to keep things light. Becoming yourself makes you momentarily the loneliest person on Earth, but as you walk through that door, you realize that you're a part of everything. And that in the end, it's impossible to be alone. That's the kind of assurance and wisdom that Nature affords: intimate knowledge of this moment, this tree, this place, this home.

DJ: And it seems to me to take a long time. I've been living on the same land now for about three years....

JWH: And you're just starting to get introduced.

DJ: Yes.

JWH: This courting and bonding requires not only commitment but presence and attention, day after day after day. If we're only home seasonally, or if we're gone five days out of the week, it's not the same. Deepening relationship requires we get to see the sun come up in a slightly different place each and every day through each of the four seasons. I've got so many friends who live in cities, who work all day indoors, and some of them don't even know which way the sun sets. Until we're oriented, until we know where we are, until we know what direction is East, how can we know what direction to take our lives? And it takes time to recognize the ecological cycles, as many of them are long. There are seven-year cycles for different insects, and there are different flowers that come up only every four to eight years. Patterns of rain and drought. New species moving in or disappearing. Miss a single week in this enchanted canyon, and you could miss the bulk of the wild mulberry season. No single sunset will ever be repeated again, quite the way it shined today.

This intimacy of relationship, this narrowing down of focus actually expands what it means to belong and to be alive. Unfortunately, such deep relating and reinhabiting can be at odds with social acceptance, producing a viable income, or covering one's medical insurance.

DJ: Why is that?

JWH: They require we do work that takes into account the integrity and needs of our bodies, our communities, other species, the air, water, and land...and that can be a hard way to make a living. The system rewards its citizens who acquiesce, compromise, and conform. We're usually paid not only to do what we're told, but to "look the other way"—away from the effects of our tasks on our bodies, our families and our world. In fact, the more meaningless or destructive the position, the more money and benefits we can make. Corporate heads and politicians, geneticists and nuclear engineers, army generals and real estate developers are highly paid. Writers and dancers, preschool teachers and counselors, environmental activists and those who run food programs for the poor, wilderness restorationists and sage poets are lucky to be paid at all. Or else they're volunteers.

But there's an upside to this. Because the fields that require caring help pay so little, they tend to attract the most sincere people. People who are doing their service for the purest of reasons. And the rewards do come, if not always in the form of cash: the fulfillment that comes with being who you really are and doing the right things. Magical connections and alliances. Heightened personal awareness and power. The timely unfolding of miracles.

DJ: What's your story?

JWH: There never really was a time when I felt like I fit in. There was never a moment I didn't feel alienated from the social agreement....

DJ: What social agreement?

JWH: That if we set aside our deepest needs, our sense of place, magic, and mission—everything will be all right, medicine will develop a cure for death, science will erect bubbles over our cities to purify the air, we'll meet Mr. or Mrs. Right. That the oil companies will come up with new forms of inexpensive energy, taking away our privacy is their way of protecting us, building more missile systems will make us safer, Social Security will really take care of us when we get old, and we can all have lots of babies with no serious effects on the environment or our quality of life. And in the end, if we play by the rules, we'll all go to heaven where there are no endangered species or slaughtered Hutu tribesmen, nor wives being beaten by husbands with no self respect.

The agreement is that we'll smile even if we don't like someone or something, and gather on Christmas and give presents even to those family members who happen to resent us the rest of the year.

That we'll ignore the child abuse we know is going on across the street, and have secretive affairs rather than be honest with our spouses about our feelings and needs. That we won't talk about the effects of the DDT we sprayed in our well-trimmed yards this afternoon, the percentage of poor, uneducated kids in the military, or the reasons for unwed mothers and chemically deformed babies. That we never consider why families looked nothing like the happy folks on TV, that no one seems to insist on a code of honor like in those Western novels, and our immediate asphalt-covered environs looked nothing like the farms, deserts, and mountains that call to us from the silver screen.

Do you remember a magazine in dentists' offices when we were kids, called *Highlights*? Do you remember the page where they'd show a picture with something out of place, like a hammer hanging from a tree, and you were supposed to figure out what was wrong with the picture? From the time I was a toddler, it's felt like that to me. It's like tapping on the rocks and discovering they're hollow, finding mold marks and seams once we look close enough at the local trees. It's like we're all living in a big theme park...and we have to pay to get out.

When I started running away from school at age 14, I found bouts of hunger more stimulating than daily doses of tasteless frozen dinners, and liked being lost better than always thinking I knew where I was going. Safety was a numbing straightjacket, so I embraced risk. I welcomed the pain, because I couldn't stomach denial anymore.

DJ: Are you talking emotional pain? Physical pain?

JWH: Both. The pain of feeling isolated and misunderstood. Of empathy—for mumbling bag ladies on the streets, Hispanics jacked up by the police, the little kids that no one takes the time to listen to. Empathy for the forests cleared, for expatriate wildlife and any seeds left crying beneath 4 inches of pavement. Even getting in fights or falling from a motorcycle had a certain refreshing honesty, functioning as a call to sensation, as adamant reminders that I was alive. Anything to know I'd escaped the paradigm of comfort, pretense, and denial.

DJ: At what point did that process of cultivating pain turn over? When did you started reaping the benefits of being present?

JWH: Immediately. It's clear that the more we're willing to feel our pain—and the agony of other people, other creatures—the greater our capacity for bliss, communion, and love. The eyes that willingly look into the faces of the suffering are more likely to notice the value of a smile, the shifting shapes in the clouds above, or the poetry of the falling leaf. Ears that find sirens unbearable can better appreciate the whisperings of the river and the quiet squeaking of grandma's rocking chair. The heart that really knows the meaning of bliss has been sensitized by despair.

DJ: Let's talk about this land [Sweet Medicine Sanctuary].

JWH: The moment I saw it, I fell helplessly in love. I sold the engine out of the school bus I lived in, in order to get the earnest money, with no idea if I could get up the rest of the down payment that I'd offered. Apparently on some of their historic raids, Vikings would find themselves suddenly outnumbered, and the chieftains would set fire to the sails knowing the men would fight harder once they saw there was no retreat. By selling the engine, I'd burned my ships, and there was no going back on my oath to purchase, protect, and be a priest to this special place.

DJ: How did you know this was the place you needed to be?

JWH: Finding our home, like finding our destiny, is a matter of getting in touch with our intuition and instinct. And then learning to trust it, and follow it. You can't pick a home by comparing the facts and maps in some atlas, any more than you can find your "medicine animals" by drawing cards from a deck. Home, like adventure, is something that becomes possible whenever we suspend our plans and criteria, and feel our way to where we most belong. It's not only the place our souls need, but also the place that most needs us. It isn't where you lay your head, it's where you pledge your heart.

The events leading me to find, buy, and preserve the Sanctuary have been nothing short of miraculous, convincing me without a doubt that I was meant to be here serving this place and teachings. And anyway, we can sense where we belong in the compass of our bones. Whenever we leave, we will feel like we're going the wrong way. And when we turn back, we know in every cell of our being that we're headed in the direction of home.

As a youngster, I preferred multiple affairs to lasting commitments, variety of experience over depth. Coming here was the end to that, the moment of pledging allegiance, of marrying the land, entering into a reciprocal agreement that demands as much from me as it gives.

DJ: You've written that we can't own land, that land owns us. What is your contract with this canyon?

JWH: How can we own that which contains us, predates us, and outlasts us? I didn't contract for this place so much as *with* it. We enter into a relationship sealed in blood and tears, sweat and semen, an equitable giving and taking that's clearly spelled out, and duly sworn to. The land is pledged to give wholly of its authentic self, to offer home and shelter, beautiful groves and stunning mountains, the food and water we need, inspiration and instruction. We promise gifts in return: our attendance and presence, attention and focus. We promise to try and feel her needs, and meet them. To support her in her fullest flowering. To defend her integrity and honor from all threats including those that come from ourselves. To appreciate, and celebrate.

It is, as much as anything else, a *marriage* contract, bound by love rather than law. I've stood before these orange and purple cliffs many times and repeated my vows. That I'll do everything I can to restore her and make her all she can be, to never bend her to my will, to always serve her, touch her, stroke her hair of grass. To revel in the sensation of my bare feet on her naked Earthen body.

DJ: This may seem strange, but when I was walking down the canyon, before I came up here to do this interview, the one thing that was missing was a lover. Had I been here with a human lover, we would have had no choice but to make love.

JWH: Of course! Everywhere we look we see an eroticized natural world both consuming itself, and making love to itself, through its constituent parts. Pollen-laden flowers pierced by wild bees. The mating calls of the sex-addled elk. Insect orgies and intertwining grape vines. We're drawn to participate in this lusting and cuddling, inspired to add our own variations of partnering and pairing. There exists what Terry Tempest Williams and I call an "erotics of place," the charged field we evolved from, and that we subconsciously long to penetrate again. Loba has joined me in making the canyon our femme paramour. You can see it in the way she touches each lichen-padded rock on the way down to the trail. The hurt look on her face if she breaks the grasses she steps on. Her look of ecstasy as the shallow river carries her slowly downstream. And the way her voice rings out on a moonlit night....

DJ: When she asked what would be required of her if she stayed with you here, one of the things you said was, "Sing praise to the canyon."

JWH: The land doesn't just need us defending it. It needs our hands-on care. Needs us to sing ritual and prayer, gratitude and celebration. From the time my sweetheart first got here, she'd stand above the river in front of a small wind cave, and sing out a cascade of trills and bars. I feel the whole canyon rising to take it in, the way a cat raises its back when you reach down to stroke it.

DJ: One of the things I love about your work is that activists generally do restoration, some Pagan types sing praises, but you do both. It's very evident how much work you've done here.

JWH: You're a gentleman for saying so. Restoration and resistance can be spiritual and art—if we infuse them with passion and prayer. Rhythm and style. Meaning and grace.

The most adamant and beautiful work in this world seems to emanate from a magical imperative, from the reptilian cortex, caring souls and expectant flesh. From Earth and Spirit. From destiny itself. It is the full-bodied, full-souled voice of the new Witches and Wizards, seers and shamans, wilders and priestesses, praise- and prayer-givers.

DJ: It's like Meister Eckhart said, if the only prayer you say in your life is "thank you," that would be sufficient.

JWH: And ideally expressed through songs, purrs, sighs, and exclamations of child-hearted amazement. Symbolic language serves only a few redeeming roles: giving thanks, giving warning, creating odes to the beloved...and directing people's attention back to what's real and wordless! If I'm constantly writing, it's only because I'm trying to pontificate others into howling, chant them into vital immediate experience. And cast the spell that can help change our world.

DJ: You write about learning from the land, and the lessons are far from the Disneyfied version where nothing or no one ever gets hurt.

JWH: Wilderness is a largely benign and beneficial experience, but it is its dangers that force us to be fully awake, to be careful, full-of-care. Our strength is a product of those challenges we pull against. Our ancestors' speedy reaction time resulted not only from running after food, but running away from trouble. The experiences that are most unforgettable are intimations of death, and reminders to live. We were never more alive, never more fully present and aware as when we were stalked by cave bears and giant cats.

Many times I've stepped a few feet off a mountain trail to let a noisy covey of hikers pass. I smile as they shuffle by staring at their feet, talking loudly about the next peak they're going to "bag," or the last woman they "had"—without them seeing me there, standing in plain sight. In grizzly country, they could end up lunch meat. It only takes one look at a grizzly's claw marks high up a tree to get us to pay a little more attention to our surroundings. Eyes alerted to spot bear tracks are more likely to notice the little flowers budding up through the clover, and the way the wind passes sensuously through the tallgrass. Ears listening intently for the sound of the great bears are more likely to hear the tinkling of a tiny rain seep, and recognize the subtleties in a river's song.

DJ: How does death fit into this picture?

JWH: Fear is a reason for increased awareness, and potentially, fuel for movement or change. In the same way, death is an ally that constantly reminds us of the real world around us, and of what's most important. If you think you only have a few weeks or months to live, you'll be unlikely to want to spend any of that time under fluorescent lights, quibbling or worrying. You'll try to spend time in your favorite places, or where you most belong. You'll revel in the moments you have with your loved ones, savor every scent and sound. But if you think you have several years left, you're likely to loiter in your mind, put off that trip to your beloved ocean or desert, suffer the cubicle lights to pull in a few more paychecks, miss precious hugs and giggles and winks with your kids and lovers. The more time you think you have, the more likely you'll postpone your spiritual work, your assignment, your purpose...the very living of life.

We already have a hard time being present and in-body—already treat the Earth as if it were a lifeless and limitless resource—knowing we're lucky if we have 70 years of relative good health. Just imagine how careless we'd be with our lives, and the lives of other species, if we could count on biomedicine to guarantee us 50 to 100 years more. Sensitivity, compassion, and gratitude are rooted in the awareness of mortality.

In this way, the big bears are our Buddhas. And viruses are agents of reconnection as well as humility.

DJ: We're not the top of the food chain.

JWH: Dirt is at the top...because it gets to eat everybody! If we really want to feel like part of the endless cycles of life, we need to get used to thinking of ourselves as food. In this society, people usually live their lives as though they were somehow separate from Nature, and then they employ embalming fluids and metal-lined coffins to try to keep Nature out after death. The late curmudgeon Ed Abbey told me he wanted his body to be laid out as a sort of cafeteria for the buzzards and coyotes. But even buried, we feed the contiguous whole that once fed us. Attempts to forestall decomposition, like science's search for immortality, signify our unwillingness to surrender to the very processes we arose from, extend out of...and all return to.

DJ: Facing death, like facing life, takes a lot of courage.

JWH: Courage is being willing to feel, no matter what the costs. And doing the right thing—acting on those feelings—in the face of every obstacle. If we are courageous, it is because we love something enough that we'd take risks to save it, help it, nourish it. The ultimate courage comes from the certain knowledge that we are an inseparable part of the Earth. We must learn to live lives that, like death, affirm the sacred connection between us and the land.

DJ: I've come to realize that there is no such thing as *anything* separate from land.

JWH: There's no such thing as *separate*. That's the whole point. Every problem in the world, every social dis-ease, every environmental imbalance, every screwed up personal problem is because we're somehow able to imagine separation between our mind and our heart, between our mind and our body, between our body and this place, between ourselves and our loved ones, ourselves and our community. There is no original evil, only original imagined separation. The cure for that is love. And the way to manifest that love is through the courageous embodiment of our decisive, magical, responsible selves. Our natural selves, in partnership with what's natural in this world.

DJ: For the longest time I tried to define what is natural, and here is what I finally came up with: an institution or rule or artifact is natural to the degree that it reinforces our understanding of our embeddedness and participation in the natural world, and it's unnatural to the degree that it masks all of that.

JWH: Exactly. And we're natural, to the degree that we embrace our embeddedness, and act out of that animal/spiritual sense of connectedness, interdependence, and inseparability...doing "the real work."

DJ: Define "the real work."

JWH: Individually making our lives a quest for reconnection, a quest for right livelihood and right living, for both meaning and beauty. This is our job—even if it were to cost our credibility or careers, the support of our parents, the acceptance of our children, or the understanding of our mates in the course of regaining our lives, our passions, our souls.

DJ: That's a hard sell.

JWH: It may always be more popular to hand out chocolate kissies and get-into-heaven-free cards, and no call to sentience and responsibility can compete with selling prayers for angels that are willing to do all the karmic work for you. New Nature Spirituality teaches that we're in charge of our own lives, and that the fate of the natural world will largely depend on what we do or don't do.

The truth can seem to "cost us everything," but it gifts us with who we really are, and gives us back the fullest experiencing of the world of which we're a part. This is insight with no borders, no convention, no pretense, no apologies. I don't ask for perfection or enlightenment from those I work with, only whole and heartful effort, a fierce focus and love. And a willingness to get up when you fall. Our Gaian teachings constitute a sort of "no ropes" course: a chance to be aware and responsible, with nothing holding you down, and the knowledge there are no nets to soften our mistakes. Instead of "12 Steps," we've narrowed it down to two: Re-become your most authentic, feeling self—and then manifest that magical self for the good of the whole. Therapists want you to have the "skills" to keep your traumas and unmet needs from interfering with your ability to "function productively" in society. I have no intention of making it easier for anyone to tolerate the hypocrisy and meaninglessness around them, or to ignore their needs and wounds. I try to give them back the will and power to resist what needs resisting, change what needs changing...and feel absolutely *all*. This is useful no matter what magical or spiritual traditions one employs, or what assignments they undertake.

Priests may absolve you, or gurus provide mantras to liberate you from your karmic cycle. Counselors may process you endlessly, without ever demanding any major shifts. Not so with the teachings of the inspirited Earth, of primal instinct and intuition...and not so with us. You can be redeemed and fulfilled, but not absolved, for the aware have a responsibility. We will ask you not to transcend but engage. And we will expect you to change—into becoming more who you really are: needy as well as giving, vulnerable as well as strong, physical as well as spiritual, angry as well as happy, determined as well as afraid. It's the least we can do.

DJ: What worries you most?

JWH: The epidemic insecurity that separativeness breeds. We're in some kind of collective denial about the fact, but there is no single greater influence on our activities, no single greater factor in the repression of our magical native humanness and the distortion and destruction of Nature. The drunk in the gutter, and the ambitious developer destroying precious wetlands, are both responding to gut-wrenching self-doubt. Those who build monumental skyscrapers, as well as those who crash planes into them, are in part compensating for the same intrinsic lack of self-worth.

The world would be a saner, healthier place if only we could learn to really, truly love ourselves. But this self-love can only come when we begin to recognize and experience our lives as truly, deeply significant. It grows proportionately with every challenge we rise to take on. It roots and strengthens with each difficult, selfless quest we see to completion. And it bears noble fruit, as we begin to fulfill our most meaningful purpose. Real self-worth is determined by our capacity to share, not by how much we own...not by the amount of practical or magical skills we have, but by the ways in which we employ them.

DJ: What about hope?

JWH: I expect nothing, and hope for miracles. I find reason for hope in Loba's unflagging compassion. In the faces of little children, the angst and anger of troubled teens, and in the determination of Zapatista women. In the efforts of American Indian traditionalists, Neo-Druids and radical Pagans, spiritual activists and environmental ethicists. In small presses and regional zines. In urban gardens, and herbicide-resistant weeds. I find hope in the insistence of my students, and the concern of our resident interns. And of course, I find it incredibly hopeful—that after the worst that technological civilization can do, life will spring back in all its diversity and glory for as long as the sun shall shine!

The only thing in the world that's truly hopeless is the person that *hopes less*! This is what keeps me speaking at any conference, church, or school that will have me, and spending so many hours of my fleeting life putting this all to paper.

DJ: Does writing help?

JWH: It helps—at least to the degree we raise a reader's awareness of the pain and bliss of life, and help incite their honorable responses. If we remind them not to let any intermediary stand between them and God, or between them and direct experience. If they're more empathetic and grateful after reading our words, more likely to dance and less likely to "sit this one out." If they cry more, laugh more, feel more. If they never knew how to have fun, and they play more afterwards. If they were never serious about anything, and they end up dealing with the really heavy stuff. If we can keep them from stubbing their toes on the same obstacles twice, and get them to chance new mistakes from which they can learn and grow. If they read about all the things we learned from a certain mulberry tree, and then go out right away and eat berries! If they're a little less tolerant of evil and the artificial, and a little more willing to take risks. If we provoke or seduce them to go barefoot, taste their food, say, "I love you" more often, or discover divine creation in even a single backyard flower.

It's an old metaphor, but we're all planting seeds. And this takes us back to the question of whether we can hope for results. A person putting out seeds can't stand around and wait and see what grows in every situation. Sometimes they might come up the first year. Others might take 10 or 15 generations, and come up when there is just enough sunshine, just enough moisture, just enough compost for the seed to sprout and bloom.

The essential task is to fully re-become who we really are, sensitives and sensualists, priestesses of delight and celebrants of life courageously opposing the destruction and lies, embracing the natural world and all its great and connective wisdom. Working and playing, loving and risking with enthusiasm and gusto! At that point there are no more quandaries, is no more need to "process," no confusion about wrong or right or wondering if we're on our path of heart. We feel, we care, and we respond with our every practiced skill, our every magical power. We express this wholeness in acts of beauty. We give no less than everything...and that, indeed, is enough.

Chapter 37

A Wizard's Counsel

You will find something more in woods than in books. Trees and stones will teach you that which you can never learn from a master.

—St. Bernard of Clairvaux

Hold fast to dreams, for if dreams die, life is a broken-winged bird that cannot fly.

—Langston Hughes

- Wizardry is not only an escape from the oppressiveness of the ordinary or "normal." It is reengagement with self and Spirit, purpose and place—the foundation of a lifelong assignment.

- Magic isn't about indulging the self, but transforming the world. Likewise, responsibility isn't obligation—it's the willingness and ability to respond.

- You have dreams you hardly share with anyone. Now it's time to live those dreams!

- Every moment is a decisive moment, and our future is a blank canvas. The only things standing in the way are those habits to which we're attached, and the fears we deny. No one is in charge of your life but you! The wand is in *your* hands....

- Having toys is not the same as having fun. Focus on sports where you actually get to play. Swim in chemical-free water, and in places where you're "not supposed to be." Walk barefoot through clover. Cry, laugh, and sing. Hug and howl!

- Nothing is accomplished by avoiding new experiences. Taste the many diverse flavors of life, being sure to spit out the bad.

- Try to remember that "making a living" isn't the same as really living. Find work that reflects not only your skills, but also your beliefs. Watching adventure stories on the screen is a poor substitute for having adventures yourself. There are just so many hours between birth and death...spend them carefully, on what matters most. Ideally, you will discover and then fulfill your most meaningful purpose.

- The point isn't to gather riches, but for us to have a richer life. Watch out for any solutions that can either be sold or bottled, and any intermediary standing between you and the experience of Gaia, God, and Goddess.

- Travel and explore as much of the world as possible. This will not only make you familiar with other bioregions and other kinds of lifestyles, but it will also help you appreciate any place you ever call home.

- Never take anything for granted—not your health, your home, or your family. Never say "whatever," because it means that you don't care, and you know very well that you do! Neither our problems nor the problems of the world, are caused by feeling too much. Rather, they're caused by us feeling too little! By opening up to the pain of conscious existence we open ourselves up to the experience of joy.

- Bravely explore anything and everything that increases the depth of sensation and the totality of Spirit, leading you through empathy into true connection and power. You are a part of the seamless universe as much as your hand is a part of your arm. All of creation is sacred, and thus so are you.

- It would be wise to avoid any drugs, careers, or lifestyles that deaden your awareness, or that impair your crucial and timely response. Be suspicious of anything that requires fossil fuels, brags about being "disposable," admits to having been artificially colored or flavored, or pretends to be something it's not. And pay attention, for goodness sake! Focus solely on your sweetheart when you're with him or her, and on no other food than that food which you're eating. Remember that nothing is worth anything, unless it's authentic!

- All events, both good and bad, are valuable lessons for which we should be grateful. Avoid stubbing your toe on the same rock twice. And don't fritter away too much precious time explaining your mistakes. Just learn from them, and go on!

- Develop a personal code of honor, and then live up to it! Promise your allegiance to your friends, your family, your community, your cause, and the land you love. And always keep your promises.

- All the world is a great gifting cycle. Learn to give all you can. And just as importantly, learn how to graciously accept every gift that comes your way.

- Take time to "be little," even if you think you're at an age when you need to be "wise" or "cool." Crawl around on the ground after interesting bugs, look for animal shapes in the clouds, and don't worry if you get grass stains on your clothes!

- Find divine creation and your place in it in every blade of grass, in every home's backyard. But don't forget to make pilgrimages to truly wild places. Open up to the information and inspiration they provide, and subject yourself to the solitude that teaches we're never truly alone.

- Expose every harmful illusion or lie. Whatever is real and good, protect and nourish with all your might.

- There is no one that will do the vital work for you, and thus there's nobody else to blame! Both the responsibilities and the rewards are yours. Take credit! Then give thanks....

- Remember that it's never "too late," so long as you start right now.

- Expect a miracle. That miracle is *you*.

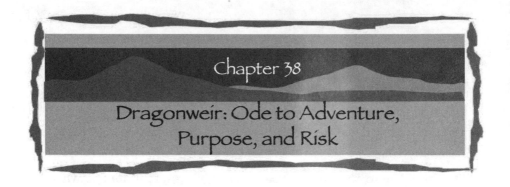

There is scarcely any passion without struggle.

—Albert Camus

*Astound me...these flashes of astonishment are what I cannot
live without.*

—Colette

Indeed—the path up the mountain is more difficult than down the valley. Yet upon reaching the top, the flowers seem more colorful, more vibrant, more alive!

There roost our dragons, their iron claws carrying us in a vise-like grip higher than ever...well worth the pain! For from such heights, all creation is visible, magic to be celebrated, differences accented, personalities sung. We revel in the rise of our eyeless ways of seeing, in our distance from the stifling gray below, in our deepening connection to all we can see and feel and know.

True satisfaction is not comfort. It is wrought with challenge and growth, variety and struggle. It is intimately, passionately, vigorously, fully experiencing life through every pore of the skin, through heart and lungs...leaving the bones trembling beneath expectant flesh!

If there were no dragons on our climb, I would create them for us—most beautiful of beasts—to test our courage, test our ability to learn from our mistakes. To stretch our potential to the limits, and then beyond. Expanding and connecting, honing our senses—an extended progression: adventure!

We are the Shaman making his fateful and dangerous climb. The Apache scout a long way between water holes. The midwife feeling in the dark of the womb for the promise of life. The Viking in uncharted waters, listening, sniffing the air for the smell of land.

Looking beyond the horizon, we know the pain of the flower longing to open, the Spirit longing to be free. We know the pain of forests being cut, of grasses screaming beneath the pavement. We feel the pain of species banished into extinction and of human potential bottled up in distraction and denial. And we feel the bliss of at last knowing there is something we can do about it.

The bells of the gypsy wagon have always called to us. Even now they are tinkling out of the darkness of human resignation and the unseen folds of the future. As we get closer, their ringing is the sound of the unchained brook, of a lover's tongue in our ear, of a hawk's cry and the whistling of the wind on highest polished cliffs. We can do nothing else but follow, nothing else but follow...in this grip of dragon-flight!

Fly!
fly!
fly!

Epilogue

"Gaia Bless"
By Jesse Wolf Hardin

Gaia Bless—
    each one of us, in our fleeting mortal moment,
    in our chance for conscious life.
    And a special blessing on those sensitive souls
    who have seen and rejected all pretense,
    even their own.
    Those who through the din
    still hear and record the instructions, the cries,
    the songs and sighs
    of the sacred Earthen Mother.
    May she be heard!

Gaia Bless—
    the bards singing of hope to the hopeless,
    poets calling forth Spirit for the godless,
    magic for the disbelieving,
    hope for the discouraged,
    joy for the dour.
    Those artists who paint so that the blind might see,
    and the old folks who talk to weeds.
    Kids who ask too many questions.
    The tribes and the tribeless.
    The happily enjoined, the seeking,
    and those contented alone.
    Those who instead plant flowers in the bulldozer's tracks,
    the willing students and committed teachers,
    the first and the last.

Gaia Bless—

    those bound to constant movement, for all the right
reasons,
riding atop tornadoes, endlessly migrating
across the wide continent of their lives...
and those who instead remain still
through the storms of transition,
who make promises,
and find ways to bond their flesh to dirt.
They who touch Her Earthen skin
just the way She likes it,
tend and finger Her willow hair.

Gaia Bless—

    us all in our heartful medicine journey,
in our willingness to feel,
in our impassioned commitment
to make our magic real.

By our hearts and our acts, may we be worthy.

Gaia Bless.
Gaia Bless.

Appendix

Suggested Further Reading

The following kindred titles reflect some of the richness of the New Nature Spirituality movement:

Abram, David. *The Spell of The Sensuous*. New York: Pantheon Books, 1996.

Adams, Cass, ed. *The Soul Unearthed*. Boulder, Colo.: Sentient, 2002.

Badiner, Allan Hunt, ed. *Dharma Gaia*. Berkeley, Calif.: Parallax Press, 1990.

Berry, Thomas. *The Dream of the Earth*. San Francisco, Calif.: Sierra Club Books, 1990.

———.*The Great Work*. New York: Harmony/Bell Tower, 2000.

Campbell, Joseph. *The Power of Myth*. Garden City, N.Y.: Anchor Books, 1991.

Devall, Bill, and George Sessions. *Deep Ecology*. Layton, Utah: Gibbs Smith, 1988.

Devall, Bill. *Simple in Means, Rich in Ends*. Layton, Utah: Gibbs Smith, 1988.

Glendinning, Chellis. *My Name Is Chellis & I'm in Recovery from Western Civilization*. Boston: Shambhala, 1994.

Halifax, Joan. *Shaman: The Wounded Healer*. New York: Crossroad/Herder & Herder, 1982.

Jensen, Derrick. *A Language Older Than Words*. New York: Context Books, 2000.

Mander, Jerry. *In the Absence of the Sacred*. Berkeley, Calif.: Sierra Club Books, 1992.

Metzner, Ralph. *The Well of Remembrance*. Boston: Shambhala, 2001.

———. *Green Psychology*. Rochester, N.Y.: Inner Traditions Int., 1999

Nollman, Jim. *Spiritual Ecology*. New York: Bantam, 1990.

Shepard, Paul. *The Others*. Washington, D.C.: Shearwater Books, 1997.

———. *Thinking Animals*. Athens, Ga.: University of Georgia Press, 1998.

Snyder, Gary. *The Practice of Wild*. New York: North Point Press, 1990.

Starhawk. *Truth or Dare*. San Francisco: Harper San Francisco, 1989.

———. *Webs of Power*. Gabriola Island, British Columbia: New Society, 2002.

Williams, Terry Tempest. *Refuge*. New York: Vintage Books, 1992.

———. *An Unspoken Hunger*. New York: Vintage Books, 1995.

———. *Coyote's Canyon*. Layton, Utah: Gibbs Smith, 1999.

Zell-Ravenheart, Oberon. *Grimoire for the Apprentice Wizard*. Franklin Lakes, N.J.: New Page Books, 2003.

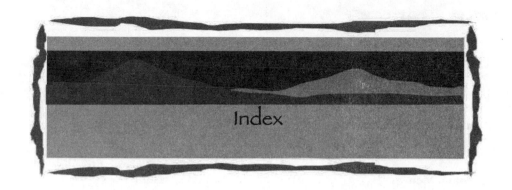

Index

About the Author

JESSE WOLF HARDIN is a renowned Gaian Wizard, contemporary spiritual teacher, artist, musician, and author of numerous books. His two decades of public appearances have helped birth both a new Gaian theosophy and ecological ethic, and have resulted in recordings of spoken word and world-beat music. Wolf's hundreds of magazine articles have united the principles of Paganism, primal mindfulness, Earthen Spirituality, and personal activism like none before. He was a core columnist for the esteemed Pagan periodical *Green Egg*, and his writing currently appears in *Magical Blend*, *Circle Nature Spirituality Quarterly*, *Elements*, *Natural Beauty & Health*, and more than a dozen regional periodicals. Most of the time, Wolf can be found at home on his enchanted New Mexico wildlife sanctuary—an ancient place of power where he teaches students and resident interns, and apprentices the art of practical magic, wildlands restoration, and Earth-centered magical practice.

Other Books by the Author

Kindred Spirits: Sacred Earth Wisdom
   (Swan•Raven 2001).

Coming Home: ReBecoming Native, Recovering Sense of Place
   (self-published).

The Kokopelli Seed: A Novel of Gaian Awakening
   (self-published).

The Gifting Bones: Tools of Perception, Tools of Choice
   (self-published, unique runic manual).

And on CD or cassette, the album of world music and spoken word: *The Enchantment* by GaiaTribe (featuring the author's spoken word invocations with canyon soundscapes and amazing world musicians).

For information on Wolf and Loba's presentations, counsel, workshops, guided quests, wilderness retreats, and resident internships, please visit *www.earthenspirituality.org*, or write:

The Earthen Spirituality Project & Sweet Medicine Women's Center
P.O. Box 820
Reserve, NM 87830